Modern
And Moral Guidance From The Sages

Jewish Ethical Wisdom From Pirkei Avot

by

Rabbi Dov Peretz Elkins

Winner of the National Jewish Book Award

Mazo Publishers

Jewish Ethical Wisdom From Pirkei Avot

ISBN 978-1-946124-79-1

Contact The Author
DPE@jewishgrowth.org

Mazo Publishers
Chaim Mazo, Publisher
Website: www.mazopublishers.com
Email: mazopublishers@gmail.com

54321

With gratitude and love

to Rabbi and Miryam Elkins,

who have helped us all become better Jews

Kim Pimley

The Author

Dov Peretz Elkins is a nationally known lecturer, educator, workshop leader, author, and book critic. He is a popular speaker on the Jewish circuit.

Rabbi Elkins is a recipient of the National Jewish Book Award, and is the author of over 55 books. His *Chicken Soup For The Jewish Soul* was on the NY Times bestseller list.

Among Rabbi Elkins' other books are *Rosh Hashanah Readings: Inspiration, Information and Contemplation, Yom Kippur Readings,* and *The Wisdom of Judaism: An Introduction to the Values of the Talmud.*

His most recent books are *To Climb The Rungs – Memoirs of a Rabbi* (Mazo Publishers), *Jewish Stories from Heaven and Earth: Inspiring Tales to Nourish the Heart and Soul, Tales of the Righteous, Simple Actions for Jews to Help Green the Planet, Heart and Scroll: Inspiring Stories from the Masters* (Mazo Publishers), *In the Spirit: Insights for Spiritual Renewal in the 21st Century, For Those Left Behind: A Jewish Anthology of Comfort and Healing* (Mazo Publishers), *A Treasury of Thoughts on Israel and Zionism* (Mazo Publishers), *The Power of Human Speech* (Mazo Publishers) and *FATE* (Mazo Publishers). See other books by Dov Peretz Elkins at www.jewishgrowth.org.

Rabbi Elkins served in several outstanding congregations in Rochester, NY, Cleveland, OH, and in Princeton, NJ, before retirement. He earned a doctorate in pastoral counseling in Rochester, NY.

Dr. Elkins lives in Jerusalem with his wife, Maxine (Miryam). They have six children and twelve grandchildren.

Contents

Endorsements 6
Acknowledgments 8
Introduction 9
Quotables 11

Pirkei Avot According To Topic Themes

Action vs. Belief 12
Anger 14
Community 18
Death 23
Empathy 25
Evil 30
Faith 32
Free Will 34
Friendship 36
God and Human Beings 40
History 44
Humans and Their Neighbors 47
Judgment 56
Kiruv (Jewish Outreach) 62
Learning and Teaching 65
Materialism 88
Mitzvot 91
Particularism vs. Universalism 95
Peace 98
Personal Qualities 101
Prayer 110
Reputation 112
Reward and Punishment 115
Self-Esteem 117
Speech and Silence 120
Tzedakah (Charity) 124
Wise People and Their Wisdom 128
Women 131
World Ethics 133
Work 142
The World-to-Come 147
Youth and Old Age 151

Glossary of Terms and Phrases 157
Bibliography 160

Endorsements

Rabbi Dov Peretz Elkins has devoted his career to collecting wisdom from the Jewish tradition and making classical and contemporary Jewish ideas accessible to learners and leaders alike.

Rabbi Lauren Berkun, Vice-President, The Hartman Institute

This is the kind of book in which you say to yourself after reading it, "Why did it take so long for someone to think of doing this?" Pirkei Avot (Ethics of the Fathers) has had centuries of commentaries, but now, for the first time, multiple commentaries on many of its passages are arranged according to topic. This will make it much more user friendly, just as the Mishnah made Jewish law more accessible by organizing it by topic. Furthermore, the wealth of commentaries that Rabbi Elkins has amassed on each topic, including classical, medieval, and modern voices, makes what the original Mishnah says all the more relevant and meaningful. We all should be grateful to Rabbi Elkins for writing this book.

Elliot Dorff, Rabbi, Ph.D., American Jewish University,
Rector and Distinguished Service Professor of Philosophy

"Find yourself a teacher," Avot advises. In these pages, I find Rabbi Dov Peretz Elkins to be an erudite and elegant teacher of Jewish ethics. Rabbi Elkins organizes *Avot* in an accessible way and provides a wealth of sources from both inside and outside of Jewish tradition to gently guide us to the ethical life.

Professor Ari L. Goldman of Columbia University,
author of "The Search for God at Harvard"

Rabbi Elkins has produced a unique commentary on a wonderful Talmudic tractate that will help all its readers derive much insight and inspiration. No commentary arranged by theme instead of chapters and Mishnayot existed until now. *Yishar koah* to Dr. Elkins for bringing to the Jewish and non-Jewish public so much profound ethical teaching from a wonderful book, Pirkei Avot.

Prof. Shalom Paul, professor emeritus and former chair,
Dept. of Bible, Hebrew University of Jerusalem

This new version of Pirke Avot has been ingeniously reorganized by subject matter for easy reference and enhanced with myriad helpful comments by the editor and by earlier readers, ancient and modern. It will be helpful to teachers and rabbis, lay readers, and anyone who seeks guidance on the good life from Jewish sources. A great idea, well carried out.

Prof. Raymond Scheindlin, professor emeritus of medieval Hebrew literature at JTS, author of "The Book of Job" and "Vulture in a Cage: Poems by Solomon Ibn Gabirol"

Acknowledgments

I want to thank the following people for their assistance in helping me make this new collection of Pirkei Avot as accurate, useful, and relevant as possible.

I am very grateful to my friend and colleague, Rabbi Charles Kraus, for verifying many of the ancient sources.

I am also grateful to my dear friend for over sixty years, Professor Shalom Paul, for his scholarly eye in making the book more accurate and readable.

Thanks to my friend Yocheved Klausner, who has improved several of my previous books, and has lent me her discerning eye in many passages in this work.

Appreciation to my dear friend Rabbi Stephen Chaim Listfield, whose careful reading of the entire manuscript has caught many typos and corrected several other errors.

I am also grateful to my dear friend Kim Pimley, for her constant support of my literary efforts and her kind friendship.

Deep appreciation to my publisher, Chaim Mazo, for his talented, skillful and artistic handling of several of my books.

Thanks to my loving wife, Miryam for her patience during my writing, and for frequent suggestions to improve my work.

Dov Peretz Elkins
Erev Rosh HaShanah, 5781
The seventy-third year of the State of Israel
Jerusalem, Israel

Introduction

We live in a broken world. We live in unprecedented times. Presidents, Prime Ministers, high level office-holders, leaders of important national and international corporations and non-profit institutions, are being accused, and often convicted, of serious crimes. In such a time, we are in need of significant wise moral guidance, and one of the most important sources of that guidance can emerge, in my view, from a little-known book embedded inside the sixty-three volume compendium known as the Talmud.

The book I refer to, Pirkei Avot, Chapters of the Sages, has been an inspiring source of ancient moral wisdom, created by many rabbis some two thousand years ago, and edited in approximately the year 200 CE. This collection has been studied, explained, interpreted and argued over for the last eighteen hundred years. Its readers have been nourished by its wisdom, inspired by its sagacity, and uplifted by its amazing insights into human behavior.

Though our rabbinic ancestors knew nothing of computers and other modern technology and science, their prescient insights into how people and society are best ordered is beyond amazing. While much has changed and evolved in the realm of science, medicine and other realms of academic knowledge, the highways and byways of the human spirit have not. Though the ancient rabbinic Sages cannot be held accountable for certain modern new ideas, such as that regarding the role of women in society, the vast majority of their insights stand firm and unchangeable. How fortunate are we that our ancestors have preserved these sagacious aphorisms for posterity.

Some will ask: Why another commentary on Pirkei Avot? I personally own scores of such commentaries, and I am certain that there are many more than I am not aware of. So how is this commentary different from others? Every commentary that I have seen is different in two important ways.

First, most commentaries place the aphorism in a historical setting. Many correctly find this information important, but my feeling is that any student can find this information in other places. I find no need to repeat the name, location, biographical background, etc. of the many authors of the wise sayings in Pirkei Avot. These important details can be found in most, or even all, of the previously published commentaries.

Second, and most important, every other commentary that I have seen is arranged according to the chapters and sentences (called Mishnayot) found in the larger body of the huge six-volume Mishnah. While many scholars have attempted to find some coherence in the ordering of these six chapters, most students find it rather difficult to see any logic or order in the five chapters (or in the sixth that was added later from a different source). What I found missing, and have attempted to supply, is a theme-based order to the collection of apothegms found in Pirkei Avot.

For example, if one attempts to find out what the Sages thought about education, or justice, or reward and punishment, it would be necessary to turn all the pages of the book to search for such attitudes. In this book, for the first time that I am aware of, all the wisdom in Pirkei Avot is arranged, not according to chapter and Mishnayot, but according to themes.

The commentaries collected arise from a smorgasbord of sources, in addition to my own thoughts and interpretations. Such ideas come from the Bible, the Talmud, the Midrash, Hasidic comments, and many other Jewish and non-Jewish sources. I have selected for inclusion a wide swath of commentators to illuminate and demonstrate contemporary relevance to the ideas included.

While not every Mishnah in the original Hebrew Pirkei Avot is included in this collection, I trust that the ones that are of vital importance to modern readers are found here.

I am hopeful that the readers of this collection will be greatly eased in their search for the ideas embedded therein.

DPE

Quotables

One who wants to be pious should observe the ideas of Tractate Avot.

Talmud, Tractate Bava Kama 30a

We owe to the Jews a system of ethics which, even if it were entirely separated from the supernatural, would be incomparably the most precious possession of mankind, worth in fact the fruits of all wisdom and learning put together. On that system and by that faith there has been built...the whole of our existing civilization.

Winston Churchill 1920

The Jews started it all – and by it I mean so many of the things we care about, the underlying values that make all of us tick, Jew and Gentile, believer and atheist. Without the Jews, we would see the world with different eyes, hear with different ears, even feel with different feelings...the role of the Jews, the inventors of Western culture, is also singular: there is simply no one else remotely like them; theirs is a unique vocation. Indeed...the very idea of vocation, of a personal destiny, is a Jewish idea.

Thomas Cahill

Every day the Torah should be in your view as new, as if you received it today at Mt. Sinai....

בכל יום יהיו בעיניך כחדשים. כאילו קבלתים היום מהר סיני.

Rashi on Deuteronomy 19:1 and 26:16

Turn it (the Torah) over and over, for everything is in it.

Pirkei Avot 5:26

Action vs. Belief

1:15 – Say little and do much.

This Mishnah may refer to those who make lots of promises and do not fulfill them. The advice is to promise less and fulfill the promise quickly and abundantly. The biblical book Proverbs (10:19) teaches: "Where there is much talking, there is no lack of transgressing, but one who curbs his tongue shows sense."

Another interpretation is to rely more on one's acts rather than on one's beliefs. Talk little about what you believe but show who you are by how you act. It's more important to walk the walk than to talk the talk. A famous passage in the Talmud puts these words into God's mouth: "If only they would ignore Me and follow My commandments." In other words it is one's actions that count, not one's beliefs. Christian doctrine dictates that there is "justification by faith." But in Judaism, as Rabbi Abraham Joshua Heschel suggests, there should be a "leap of action" rather than a "leap of faith." [(1)] The famous sage Rabbi Akiva taught that "Everything is according to the preponderance of action" (3:19).

In a much later midrash on Avot, [(2)] the author compares two people from Tanakh – one who said little and did much, and the other who said much and did little. The first is Abraham who promised the angels a morsel of bread [(3)] and presented them with a sumptuous feast. On the other hand, Ephron the Hittite promised to donate to Abraham a field and a cave within in to bury Sarah, [(4)] but soon after told him it would cost a small fortune. Ephron promised a lot, and gave little.

The Talmud, in a later passage, emphasizes this point: "The righteous promise little and perform much, the wicked promise much and perform not even a little". [(5)] In its typical hyperbolic fashion, that Midrash teaches that "Whoever learns Torah but does not practice it,

1 Commonly attributed to Christian theologian Soren Kierkegaard
2 *Avot d'Rabbi Natan*, 7th to 9th century
3 Genesis 18:15
4 Genesis 23:11-15
5 Bava Metzia 87a

it would have been better if he had never been born." [6]

A third interpretation from the commentary Magen Avot [7] adds this thought: When someone plans to do a mitzvah, he should not announce it in advance. This often causes his plan to collapse. If, on the other hand, one does not announce it but actually does it, he will probably succeed.

Another explanation of the importance of action is offered by Maimonides: [8] Commenting on Avot 3:19, "everything depends on the abundance of good deeds," he teaches that what really counts is the number of good deeds one performs. It is better to give many small donations of charity to many individuals, instead of giving one large donation to one individual.

Good character is seen by habit. The more one does good deeds, the more likely will the habit be ingrained and the person's character improved.

Rabbi Murray Stadtmauer wrote this, which is a clear example of how one follows this advice in our own lives: "In my career as a rabbi, I always felt I was carrying a burden of social responsibility. People watch us, and may very well learn more from what we do than what we say."

How often do we hear the plaintive cry, "Yeah, he talks a good game, but..."

And the Gemara says it, too. *Yesh na'eh doresh v'ain na'eh mekayem* ("One may preach well and yet not do well"). [9]

And we also find it in the Mittel-Hokh Deutsch I used to hear from my dear late mother, who lived in Dresden before coming to America:

> "Vie mankher preidikt ois der Bibel,
> "Und lebt dokh zo Ebil." [Note the rhyme.]
>
> "See how one preaches from his Bible,
> "And yet leads a life of Evil."

Or if you wish to hear it from the Romans: *moribus non semper consonant oratio* ("our talk is not always consistent with what we do"). So, sure, say it. But, above all, make sure you do it!

---

6 Midrash Rabbah 35:7

7 Rabbi Shimon ben Zemah Duran, Livorno, d. 1444

8 d. 1204, Egypt

9 Tractate Hagigah 14b

Anger

2:15 – Do not anger easily.

An excellent discussion of all aspects of anger can be found in the Wikipedia article on anger. Likewise *The Jewish Encyclopedia* has a full article by the well-known Rabbi Kaufmann Kohler. The dangers of uncontrolled anger are listed by ancient philosophers Galen and Seneca, who regarded it as a kind of madness. "They all rejected the spontaneous, uncontrolled fits of anger and agreed on both the possibility and value of controlling anger." On the other hand, Aristotle ascribed a certain value to anger that comes from perceived injustice.

The Torah evidences many comments on anger. Father Jacob condemned his sons Simon and Levi: "Cursed be their anger so fierce; and their wrath so cruel". (1) Even Israel's greatest prophet, Moses, known to be the most humble of all people, expressed anger. (2)

The biblical book of Proverbs (16:32) teaches: One who is slow to anger is better than a strong man, and one who masters his passions is better than one who conquers a city."

And also in Proverbs 29:22, "an angry person provokes a quarrel, and one possessed by rage brings much sin."

The Talmud condemns spontaneous anger in strong terms: "Rabbi Yonatan said: Anyone who gets angry, all kinds of Gehenna [hell] rule over him, because anger causes him to transgress by all kinds of severe sins."

In another oft-quoted passage, the Talmud (3) warns that there are three typical ways that a person displays his/her true personality: In Hebrew alliteration: *keeso, koso, kaaso,* (his wallet, his cup and his anger) or by the way we give charity, how we drink, and how we show anger. The Maharsha, (4) one of the great 16th-century commentators on the Talmud, writes that these three – cup, wallet

1 Genesis 49:7
2 Numbers 31:14
3 Eruvin 65b
4 Rabbi Shmuel Eidels, Poland, d. 1631

and anger – indicate how a person rates in the three most important relationships he has in life: his relationship to himself, to others, and to God, respectively. If he cannot control his liquor, it means that he has not found the proper balance between his physical and spiritual sides, and has no self-control. If he doesn't share his money with others who are less fortunate, this reflects negatively on his relationship with the world around him. And finally, if he loses his temper too often, he obviously suffers in his relationship with God, as he thinks that he is God, and everything should go the way he wants it, or else he gets angry.

And this: "Anyone who is angry…their wisdom runs away from them".

In the early Middle Ages, the Zohar [5] (1:27) warns, "One who is angry is as though he worshiped idols," following an earlier Talmudic teaching that "Rabbi Yoḥanan ben Nuri: One who rends his garments in anger, or who breaks vessels in anger, or who scatters money in anger, should be like an idol worshiper in your eyes, as that is the craft of the evil inclination." [6]

In its section dealing with ethical traits a person should adopt, the *Kitzur Shulhan Arukh* (29:4) states: "Anger is a very evil trait, and it should be avoided at all costs. One should train oneself not to become angry even if he has a good reason to be angry."

In more recent times, Rabbi Shmuley Yanklowitz quotes Rabbi Samson Raphael Hirsch: "Rather than feeling anger at your friend's conduct, think of your own shortcomings and work unceasingly at the improvement of your own character." [7]

How do we control our anger? As in so many places in rabbinic tradition, we are told to model our character after God, who is "slow to anger". [8] As the Psalms (30:5) teach us: "God's anger is but for a moment, but His favor lasts a lifetime."

Rabbi Abraham Joshua Heschel wrote: "The anger of God is not a blind explosive force operating without reference to the behavior of man, but rather voluntary and purposeful, motivated by concern for right and wrong."

---

5 Book of medieval mysticism

6 Tractate Shabbat 105b

7 Pirkei Avot: A Social Justice Commentary, p.103

8 Exodus 34:6

Is all anger harmful and evil? Not at all. Anger is necessary to end injustice. Righteous indignation is an important moral trait. Hasidic masters teach that anger should not be avoided, but redirected and channeled toward healthy and ethical objectives. Remember that the Mishnah in Avot tells us not to anger easily; it does not say "never" get angry.

Rabbi Yechiel Eckstein wrote this about anger: An old Jewish folktale tells a story about a man who showed his father great respect and did whatever his father asked of him. When his father was on his deathbed, he said to the son, "Just as you honored me during my lifetime, continue to do so after my death by obeying these instructions: When you grow angry, refrain from taking action until the next day."

After his father died, the man left for a business trip that lasted many years. Unbeknownst to him, his wife was pregnant when he left. When the man returned from his trip, he heard a young man in his home conversing and laughing with his wife. He immediately assumed that his wife had been unfaithful in his absence and felt his anger flare. He drew his sword in order to slaughter the man in his home, but then remembered the promise he had sworn to his father – not to act immediately on anger – and put his sword away.

A few minutes later the man heard his wife say to the stranger in the house, "Had your father known you were born, he would already be finding you a good wife." The man suddenly realized that the person he almost murdered out of anger was indeed his son. He greeted his wife and his son and blessed God who helped him control his fury, saving him from making the biggest mistake of his life. This story has been passed down for generations in order to illustrate the danger of acting in anger.

The Talmud teaches: "When a person gives in to anger, if he is wise, his wisdom leaves him. If he is a prophet, his power of prophecy leaves him; if greatness was decreed for him from Heaven, anger will cause him to be degraded." Anger hurts no one more than the person who experiences it.

In Proverbs we read: "A person's wisdom yields patience; it is to one's glory to overlook an offense." Literally translated from the original Hebrew, the verse begins, "A person's wisdom makes him slow to anger..." Either way, the verse is understood as a teaching on anger. If we are wise, we will avoid it at all costs.

One of the greatest causes of anger is when a person feels slighted. The second part of the verse teaches us that to become angry doesn't increase our honor; rather, when we are able to let offenses pass, we will be honored. Those who act out rashly in anger do nothing to win the respect of others. However, when we can keep a cool head and act intelligently and in a dignified manner, we will earn the respect of all.

Rabbi David Wolpe teaches this lesson on the dangers of anger: In an angry age, may we say a word against anger? "Every person who becomes angry, even if a sage, his wisdom departs from him. If he is a prophet, his prophecy departs from him."[9]

There are many reasons to be angry in this world, and to feel anger at injustice is a natural and salutary thing. But to act in anger or to express yourself when angry is far more likely to be destructive than productive. Expressing anger rarely quenches it – it generally increases it. As the old saying has it, the only people who hear both sides of a family argument are the people in the next house.

Anger, our Sages teach us, is like a boiling pot – it spills over into other things. The least controllable of emotions, it convinces us of its own justification. We may doubt why we are sad, or even happy; few people can feel doubts when in the grip of anger.

If sages lose their wisdom and prophets their prophecy, what do ordinary people lose from anger? – their judgment and capacity to listen. Be angry; but wait until it subsides to act. Rage feels good but right feels better.

This Mishnah (5:14) is self-explanatory: "There are four types of temperament:

> *(1) One who is easily angered and easily pacified – his loss is canceled by his gain.*
>
> *(2) One who is hard to anger and hard to pacify – his gain is canceled by his loss.*
>
> *(3) One who is hard to anger and easily pacified is pious.*
>
> *(4) One who is easily angered and hard to pacify is wicked."*

9 Pesahim 66b

Community

2:5 – Do not separate yourself from the community.

Jews have lived in community from the beginning of our history. Some call Jews a nation, some call us a people, some call us a culture. In any case, a Jew cannot survive as a Jew without community.

After the family, community takes the primary place for Jewish religious observance and study. The synagogue, a Greek word meaning a place for gathering, is where Jews pray, study and socialize. These three components are the activities that take place in what is called in Hebrew *Bet Knesset. Bet Knesset* has three functions: *Bet Tefilah* (House of Prayer), *Bet Midrash* (House of Study) and *Bet Knesset* (a tautology, of course, but this part gives it name to the entire institution) – House of Gathering.

When Jews moves to a new city, the first thing they seek is proximity to a synagogue. Jews prefer to live where there are other Jews, with whom they can share religious, intellectual, cultural and social life. They want a place where, if they have children, they can bring their family to learn about Jewish tradition, and celebrate life cycle milestones. The synagogue has been the heart of communal life, and the setting for all its activities. According to Dr. Philip Birnbaum, "…no human institution has a longer continuous history than the synagogue, and none has done more for the uplifting of the human race." [1]

Many of the most important prayers in the traditional liturgy can be recited only in a quorum of ten adults. Important family celebrations, such as bar and bat mitzvah, weddings, and more and more today, funerals, take place in the synagogue. Often the first question a Jew asks another Jew at a first meeting will be "What synagogue do you belong to?"

When we recite the prayer for healing in the synagogue, we not only mention the name of those who are ill, but we add the phrase "among all those who are ill." When we extend comfort to a mourner, we not only ask God to comfort the mourner, but we

1 Encyclopedia of Jewish Concepts

add the phrase, "among all the mourners for Zion and Jerusalem."

If we go back to the beginning of the creation of the world, what do we find when Adam is created and has no one else to be with, talk to, share his life with? "The Lord God said: 'It is not good for man to be alone'". [(2)] The fear of being alone is a ubiquitous phenomenon in the world today. Even people who have multiple "friends" on Facebook and other social media, still feel the need for community. Internet friends do not provide the warmth, the intimacy, the caring and the hugging, that real-time friends in a close-knit community can provide.

There is a poignant story in the Talmud about a certain man named Honi the Circle-Drawer. [(3)]

One day he was journeying on the road and he saw a man planting a carob tree; he asked him, "How long does it take [for this tree] to bear fruit?"

The man replied, "Seventy years."

He then further asked him, "Are you certain that you will live another seventy years?"

The man replied, "I found [ready grown] carob trees in the world, as my forefathers planted these for me, so I too plant these for my children."

Honi sat down to have a meal and sleep overcame him. As he slept, a rocky formation enclosed upon him which hid him from sight and he continued to sleep for seventy years. When he awoke, he saw a man gathering the fruit of the carob tree and he asked him, "Are you the man who planted the tree?"

The man replied, "I am his grandson." Thereupon he exclaimed: "It is clear that I have slept for seventy years."

He then returned home and inquired, "Is the son of Honi the Circle-Drawer still alive?"

The people answered him, "His son is no more, but his grandson is still living."

Thereupon he said to them, "I am Honi the Circle-Drawer" – but no one would believe him.

He then went to the *Bet Midrash* and overheard the scholars say, "The law is as clear to us as in the days of Honi the Circle-Drawer,

---

2 Genesis 2:18

3 Tractate Taanit 23a

for whenever he came to the *Bet Midrash*, he would settle for the scholars any difficulty that they had."

Whereupon he called out, "I am he," but the scholars would not believe him nor did they give him the honor due to him. This hurt him greatly and he prayed [for death] and he died.

Raba said: Hence the saying, "Either companionship or death."

The Talmud has these teachings about the importance of living in community: [4]

"One who does not join the community in times of danger and trouble will never enjoy the Divine blessing."

And: "When the Jewish people are in trouble and one of them withdraws from the community, the two ministering angels who accompany every person come and place their hands on his head and say: 'May this one who withdrew from the community not live to see the comfort of the community.'"

The Hebrew word for community, *tzibbur* is composed of three Hebrew root letters – *tzadi*, *bet, resh*, which can be an acronym for *tzaddik* (righteous), *beinoni* (moderate), and *rasha* (evil), implying that a *tzibbur*, a community, must include everyone from the righteous, to the moderate person, to the evil one.

In the Passover Seder, one of the four children, the *rasha*, [the evil one] is so called because he excludes himself from the community. Nevertheless he is included in the Seder.

In the Talmud we read that Rabbi Shimon Ḥasida says: "Any fast that does not include the participation of some of the sinners of the Jewish people is not a fast." [5]

Maimonides, who lived about a thousand years later, expressed the idea in these words: "By virtue of his nature, man seeks to form communities."

An eloquent modern rabbi, Wayne Dosick, expressed the need for community in this way:

"In community, there is shared memory, unity of purpose, mutual commitment, reciprocal responsibility, and common destiny.

"In community, there is powerful energy that heightens awareness, supports unfolding consciousness, strengthens cosmic connection, enhances prayer, deepens meditation, and affirms

4 Tractate Taanit 11a

5 Tractate Keritot 6b

transcendent experience.

"In community there is sharing of tragedy amid triumph – joy enhanced, sorrow eased.

"In community, there is support for personal healing – the pain and sufferings of physical disease and emotional trauma are tempered and soothed.

"In community there is encouragement and energy for global healing – the task of transforming and perfecting the world is advocated and empowered."

A clever management consultant taught his students about the importance of working in tandem. He wrote this clever description of how geese organize a community for mutual protection. It may or may not be scientifically correct, but it teaches some important lessons about the need for community:

The Geese and Us

"As each bird flaps its wings, it creates an uplift for the bird immediately following. By flying in a "V" formation, the whole flock adds at least 71% more flying range than possible if each bird flew on its own."

People who share a common direction and sense of community can get where they are going more quickly and easily because they are traveling on the thrust of one another.

"When a goose falls out of formation, it suddenly feels the drag and resistance of trying to go it alone ... and quickly gets back into formation to take advantage of the lifting power of the bird in front.

If we have as much sense as a goose, we will stay in formation with those who are headed the same way.

"When the head goose gets tired, it rotates back in the wing and another goose flies point."

It is sensible to take turns doing demanding jobs, whether with people or with geese flying south.

"Geese honk from behind to encourage those up front to keep up their speed."

What do we say when we honk from behind?

"Finally – and this is important – when a goose gets sick or is wounded by gunshot and falls out of formation, two other geese fall out with that goose and follow it down to lend help and protection.

They stay with the fallen goose until it is able to fly or until it dies. Only then do they launch out on their own or with another formation to catch up with their group."

If we have the sense of a goose, similarly, we also will stand by each other.

The English poet, William Blake (1757-1827), sums it up:

I looked for my soul, but my soul I could not see
I looked for my God, but my God eluded me
I looked for a friend, and there I found all three.

Death

2:5 – Do not believe in yourself until the day you die.

2:15 – Repent one day before your death.

4:4 – Be extremely humble of spirit, for the end of a mortal is the worm (the grave).

Maimonides warns that no one should be so self-confident in his/her positive ethical traits until the end of life. We can all fall back on bad habits at any time. Other commentaries point out that Yohanan served as Kohen Gadol, the High Priest, for eighty years, but towards the end of his life, he became a Sadducee.[1]

A good trait, teaches Maimonides, must be practiced over and over, or one might lose it. Life consists of constant self-improvement. No one should be satisfied with his present moral development. "One who does not increase, decreases."[2]

Other commentaries, illustrating the unpredictability of the future, point out that financial or professional success is often not permanent. Look at what happened with the Ponzi scandal when Bernie Madoff helped scores of people become millionaires, only to discover in the end that it was all fake, and their wealth diminished severely. Even King Solomon, according to one tradition, was temporarily dethroned in his old age.

Every person is born with two inclinations, the *Yetzer HaTov* (positive inclination) and the *Yetzer HaRa* (evil inclination). One should never assume that the *Yetzer HaRa* has been defeated permanently. About King Solomon it is written, "In his old age, his wives turned away Solomon's heart after other gods, and he was not wholeheartedly devoted to the Lord his God as his father David had been."[3]

Some commentaries emphasize the word "yourself" ("Do not believe in yourself…."), meaning that everyone must believe that others are there to help, advise, support. One who thinks she/he can do it all alone is mistaken. No one can achieve anything important

1 Tractate Berakhot 29a

2 Avot 1:13

3 I Kings 11:4

without the help of others.

Regarding the advice to "repent one day before death," – we find this teaching in the Talmud: Rabbi Eliezer's students asked him: But does a person know the day on which he will die? He said to them: All the more so this is a good piece of advice, and one should repent today lest he die tomorrow; and by following this advice one will spend his entire life in a state of repentance. (4)

Knowing that we all die should make us humble. No matter how famous, wealthy or successful, we all have the same end, "for the end of a mortal is the worm (the grave)."

Rabbi Berel Wein writes: "The Jewish view of balance and reality remains the only intelligent and positive view of human mortality and productivity, coupled with the realization of the inevitability of death. The Torah bids us to choose life, and to live it fully, all the while knowing that we are mortal and temporary creatures."

---

4 Tractate Shabbat 153a

Empathy

2:5 – Do not judge your friend until you have reached his place.

Rashi [1] comments: "Do not harshly condemn someone who surrendered to temptation until, presented with a similar temptation, you conquered it." This advice is wise and humane. It suggests developing a sense of carefully achieved empathy before passing judgment on another person.

Empathy is the experience of appreciating someone's thoughts, feelings and circumstances from her or his point of view, rather than from one's own. This helps people behave in a more compassionate manner. Empathy is different from sympathy. Sympathy is feeling sorrow or pity for the difficulties that another faces, while empathy is placing oneself in the position of another, something that actors must learn in order to be successful in their craft.

Other cultures have similar advice. Counsel often attributed to various Indian tribes actually comes from a poem by Mary T. Lathrap in 1895 – called "Judge Softly."

Pray, don't find fault with the man who limps or stumbles along the road, unless you have worn the moccasins he wears, or stumbled beneath the same load.

There may be tears in his soles that hurt, though hidden away from view. The burden he bears, placed on your back, may cause you to stumble and fall, too.

Don't sneer at the man who is down today, unless you have felt the same blow that caused his fall or felt the shame that only the fallen know.

You may be strong, but still the blows that were his, unknown to you in the same way, may cause you to stagger and fall, too.

Don't be too harsh with the man that sins or pelt him with words, or stone, or disdain, unless you are sure you have no sins of your own, and it's only wisdom and love that your heart contains.

For you know if the tempter's voice should whisper as soft to

1 Acronym for Rabbi Shlomo Yitzhaki, Troyes, France, d. 1105

you, as it did to him when he went astray, it might cause you to falter, too.

Just walk a mile in his moccasins before you abuse, criticize and accuse. If just for one hour, you could find a way to see through his eyes, instead of your own muse.

I believe you'd be surprised to see that you've been blind and narrow minded, even unkind. There are people on reservations and in the ghettos who have so little hope, and too much worry on their minds.

Brother, there but for the grace of God go you and I. Just for a moment, slip into his mind and traditions and see the world through his spirit and eyes before you cast a stone or falsely judge his conditions.

Remember to walk a mile in his moccasins and remember the lessons of humanity taught to you by your elders. We will be known forever by the tracks we leave in other people's lives, our kindnesses and generosity.

Take the time to walk a mile in his moccasins.

Rabbi Ovadiah of Bartenura [(2)] taught that when one sees another person unable to withstand temptation, it is important to withhold judgment until one is faced by the same circumstances and overcomes the test.

In two stories in Genesis, we read that God "went down" to see what happened: the story of the Tower of Babel, and the story of the wickedness of Sdom and Amorrah.

Rashi, echoing many other commentators and referencing the Midrash Tanhuma says, He really did not need to do this, but Scripture intends to teach judges and magistrates that they should not proclaim a defendant guilty before they have examined a situation and thoroughly understand the matter in question.

Rashi could also have pointed out that if God needs to "go down and see" what happened, before making judgment, how much more so must we, flesh and blood, "go down" and investigate, and put ourselves in others' space before passing judgment.

In Rashi's view Moses exhibits great empathy:

2 15th century, Italy

"After some time, Moses grew up, and he went out to his people and saw their burdens." [3]

Many comments in the Midrash and in Rashi are based on tiny linguistic and grammatical wrinkles. If one reads this verse literally, it says in Hebrew that Moses saw "*b-sivlotam*," or "he saw *in* their burdens. Rashi assumes, based on Midrash Shemot Rabbah 1:27, that Moses focused his eyes and his heart on what he saw, and was distressed over the burdens of his people. It is one thing to "see" their burdens, and yet another to see, feel and empathize with them. That is the meaning that Rashi infers from the Torah. This tells us about the connection that Moses had with his people, and the immediate response he had when he saw that they were enslaved and suffering. It also tells us about the kind of person Moses was – not one who could go back to the luxury of Pharaoh's palace and ignore the pain of his people.

The following Hasidic story illustrates very well the dangers of lack of empathy: [4]

The Sin was Atoned

A certain man desecrated Shabbat accidentally, because his wagon broke down on the road on the eve of Shabbat, and he arrived at the city after candle lighting time. The man went to Rabbi Mikhal of Zlotchov to ask him for a reparation for the desecration of Shabbat. Rabbi Mikhal arranged for a harsh act of repentance, according to what is written in the books, to fast a long time and to roll in snow and sit in cold water in the winter beneath the ice.

The man began to perform these harsh acts of mortification, and he saw that he could not perform them due to the weakness of his body. He was deeply pained. At the same time the Baal Shem Tov (Besht) came to town to hear the man who was repenting.

The sinner traveled to see the Besht and asked him for a repair for his desecration of Shabbat. The Besht ordered him to take a package of candles to light in the synagogue in honor of Shabbat, and this will be his repair. The man was frightened and said to the

---

3 Exodus 2:11

4 Simcha Raz, *Stories of the Baal Shem Tov,* translated by Dov Peretz Elkins

Besht: "Is it possible that a small repair like this will atone for the desecration of Shabbat? Rabbi Mikhal of Zlotchov gave me a very strong recipe of repair. Woe is me; I do not have strength to fulfill it."

The Besht said: "Do not fear, Reb Yid, do as I told you, and you will have complete atonement."

He did what the Besht said, bought a pack of candles and went happily to the synagogue. He did not find the shamash, so he left the candles on the desk and went about his business.

A dog came into the synagogue, jumped on the pulpit and ate the candles. The man saw that his gift was consumed by the dog, and his heart was greatly pained.

Again he went to the Besht and told him what had happened, that the dog ate the object of mending the sin.

The Besht said to him: "Nevertheless, do not worry about it. Go again and buy another package of candles and give them to the shamash to light them in honor of Shabbat, and you will have atonement. And tell Rabbi Mikhal in my name, that I order him to come to me to spend next Shabbat with me."

The man went to Rabbi Mikhal and gave him the message about the order of the Besht.

Rabbi Mikhal got into his wagon and traveled to the town. On his way, near the city, the wheel of the wagon broke and Rabbi Mikhal was forced to continue on foot. While walking, it began to get dark, and he arrived at the place quite a while after the beginning of Shabbat.

When he entered the inn of the Besht, the Besht was already about to make Kiddush over the wine. He greeted Rabbi Mikhal and said to him in these words: "Rabbi Mikhal, from now on you should know, that one does not give a harsh repair like this to one who desecrates Shabbat in error. You, Rabbi Mikhal, have not experienced a sin in your lifetime, and you do not know what a broken heart of a Jew feels like, a Jew who accidentally sinned, Heaven forbid. Because of this you are not suited to pronounce a harsh decree of repentance on a Jew. You should know, Rabbi Mikhal, that through a broken heart, which this Jew who desecrated Shabbat had, he has already atoned for his sin, and it is totally erased."

In *Mahzor Vitry*, compiled by Simhah ben Shmuel, a French

Talmudist (d. 1105) and student of Rashi, we find this comment: "When King Solomon completed the building of the Bet Mikdash (the holy Temple of Jerusalem), he put the keys under his pillow. One of his wives deceived him into oversleeping, thus missing the morning sacrifice. When the idolater Jeroboam rebuked King Solomon, a Heavenly voice pronounced: 'Evil one, Jeroboam, Solomon is an unintended sinner, while you are a defiant idolater.' This is a prominent example of judging a person without having been in his situation."

Another interesting interpretation of this Mishnah comes from Menahem Meiri: [5] Focusing on the words "his place," he suggests that the intent here is that one must not judge another when he is far from home, when people make efforts to create a good impression. Thus, one can only judge another when he is near his home surroundings, when he is in his natural condition, his guard is down, exhibiting his real self.

Dennis Prager, in his commentary on the verse in Exodus 22:20, "You shall not wrong a stranger or oppress him, for you were strangers in the land of Egypt," [6] writes: "Given the unique power of empathy to lead to moral behavior, it is incumbent on all of us to aspire to empathy. Empathy is so important it might well be the solution to the problem of human evil. If people identified with others, they would no longer find it easy to inflict suffering on them, or to ignore the suffering of others."

Philosopher Hannah Arendt warned "the death of human empathy is one of the earliest and most telling signs of a culture about to fall into barbarism."

5 Spain, d. 1306

6 Exodus, Regnery Faith, 2018, pp. 325-6

Evil

4:19 – It is not in our power to explain either the peace of the wicked or the suffering of the righteous.

Over the years many people have asked me, in my capacity as a rabbi and proponent of Jewish theology, why does God let terrible things happen to good people? There are several book-length treatments to deal with this subject. This thorny question has puzzled humans as far back as the biblical book of Jeremiah (12:1), "Why does the way of the wicked prosper? Why are the workers of treachery at ease?" In another biblical book, that of Job, the entire book seems to refute the idea that pain is the result of Divine punishment. This problematic question surely has been raised even before the days of the Bible. The statement in Avot that we study now, suggests that it is not in our hands to offer a good answer.

Before delving into some of the answers proffered by ancient, medieval and modern commentators, I want to relate the few brief replies that I have given to congregants of mine, and to anyone else who asked.

The first and most important answer that I offer is that this question has stumped brilliant theologians from time immemorial. Thus, far be it from me to find an answer that is new, or, indeed, satisfying, after millennia of incomplete replies. We read in the Book of Exodus, that Moses only saw God's back (33:23); even our greatest prophet was not permitted to understand the mysteries of the Divine.

After this feeble defense, I then suggest a few inadequate, but nevertheless reasonable replies, which is all I can do. One is the reply given by Rabbi Joseph B. Soloveitchik, who wisely suggests that instead of finding a rational explanation, we should try to alleviate suffering. Focusing too much on answers will prevent us from doing what must be done – to help and support those who are in pain. A similar answer is given by my colleague Rabbi Harold Kushner, which is that God is not in the deadly automobile accident, God is in the ambulance. In other words, God does not bring evil upon good people, but God is there to comfort them, support them, and empathize with them. As the Psalmist wrote (91:15): "I will be with him in distress."

Another suggestion I have offered is that if God intervened in human behavior every time a good person faced a threat, there would be no such thing as free will. What makes human beings moral creatures is that they have the choice to do good or evil in the world.

The Torah advises, "I have set before you life and death, blessings and curses. Now choose life." [1] If God makes all our decisions, there can be no moral choice. The Torah tells us to choose life, confirming that it is in human power to make moral choices. When evil occurs, it is not God's action, it is the evil choice of human beings.

These answers are not perfect, but they do satisfy me, and hopefully some of the others to whom I offered them.

Rabbi Yisrael Salanter [2] taught that not knowing why evil occurs is not an excuse to sit back and ignore others' suffering. He wrote: "Do not say that what God has made cannot be altered – and that because the Blessed One has planted within me an evil force, I cannot hope to uproot it. This is not so, for the powers of a human being may be subdued, and even transformed. Humanity has the power to subdue its own evil nature, and to change its nature toward the good, through exercise and practice."

The late American rabbi, Milton Steinberg, [3] made this profound analysis. A believer has to account for the existence of evil and unjust suffering. The atheist has to explain everything else.

---

1 Deuteronomy 30:19
2 Lithuania, d. 1883
3 New York, d. 1950

Faith

2:19 – Know how to answer a heretic. Know for whom you labor and who is your Employer, who will pay you the reward of your work.

Faith can be defined in many ways. This Mishnah suggests that one must be prepared to respond to one without faith – a heretic – or, better, one who objects to faith in God. Judaism is a religion of deeds and belief. Belief is faith in God and in the goodness of creation. What is not recommended here is blind faith. Since Judaism believes in the human ability to reason, to use the Divine gift of a mind, a rational brain, the faith of a Jew should be a faith that does not contradict reason. Rabbi Hayyim of Volozhin [1] told his students never to accept anything from their teachers unless they understood it. Judaism, in his view, must be understood, not accepted on blind faith.

Rabbi Shmuley Yanklowitz wisely suggests that maintaining faith requires three elements: Being prepared for external challenges, keeping ever conscious of the Divine, and remembering that there is a God of justice who is in control of the universe. These three elements correspond to the three parts of our Mishnah. When one has strong faith in what s/he believes, it is obviously easier to defend the faith against attack by a heretic.

The Hebrew word for faith is "emunah," the literal meaning of which is "support." One who has faith, has trust in the support of God; namely that God created the universe. That our world is not an accident or totally random. To me this is the best answer to a heretic. How much of a difficulty it would be to think that our complex universe and all its creatures are the random accident of a "big bang." A Jew should be prepared to deliver such an argument against those with no faith. One with faith believes that the universe was created and is supported by God.

The Talmud relates an example of debating with a non-believer. [2] The emperor (Hadrian) said to Rabbi Yehoshua ben Ḥananya: I wish to see your God.

1 Belarus, d. 1821

2 Hullin 59b-60a

Rabbi Yehoshua said to him: You cannot see Him.

The emperor said to him: Truly, I wish to see Him.

Rabbi Yehoshua went and stood the emperor facing the sun in the season of Tammuz, i.e., summer. Rabbi Yehoshua said to him: Look at it.

The emperor said to him: I cannot [The light blinded him].

Rabbi Yehoshua said to him: Now, if with regard to the sun, which is only one of the servants that stand before the Blessed Holy One, you say: I cannot look at it, is it not all the more so with regard to the Divine Presence?

"Know for whom you labor." Rabbi Ovadiah Bartenura [3] comments that when one has complete faith in God, s/he can then argue with confidence with a heretic. Know for whom you labor, and strengthen your faith in God, so you are conversant with your claims.

One final comment. While being a heretic, a non-believer in God, is surely objectionable, the Hasidic master, Rabbi Simhah Bunim, suggests that on certain occasions it is desirable to be a non-believer. He says, "When a poor person requests tzedakah, it is not a good idea to think that God will take care of him. Better to act as if there is no God, and be the person who takes care of the indigent individual."

3 Italy, d. 1515

Free Will

3:19 – All is foreseen, yet freedom of choice is given. The world is judged with goodness, but all depends on the majority of one's deeds.

In the previous comment on "Evil," we discussed the importance of the idea that humans have free will, making them moral creatures. If there was no choice between acting in a moral way or an immoral way, there could be no possibility of a moral human being. When we raise the question whether God knows what our choices will be, there is an apparent contradiction. If God knows what choices we will make, how can we say that we have free will? This Mishnah explains that the two ideas co-exist: God's foresight and absolute human free will. How can Divine omniscience and human moral agency co-exist? How do we reconcile these two seemingly contradictory ideas? Let's examine some possibilities.

Philosopher Immanuel Kant[1] suggests that the two ideas cannot be reconciled. Our Mishnah disagrees. We indeed have free choice in our behavior, but God knows what choices we will make. God does not determine our choices, but He knows what they will be. A puzzlement!

Rabbi Irving (Yitz) Greenberg makes the fascinating comment that our Mishnah "illustrates the richness and pluralism of rabbinic thinking." In other words, the Sages are not afraid to tackle issues that seem difficult to reconcile. My late teacher, Prof. Louis Finkelstein, taught our class that in the view of the Talmud, two opposite views can co-exist, affirming what Greenberg wrote, that Judaism is a broad tent, and has room for wide differences of opinion. In the classic rabbinic view, "Both these and these are the words of the living God."[2]

This verse in the Torah affirms our free will:[3] "I call heaven and earth to witness against you this day, that I have set before you life and death, the blessing and the curse. Therefore choose life."

1 Germany, d. 1804
2 Tractate Eruvin 13b
3 Deuteronomy 30:19

Maimonides, the giant of medieval Judaism, believed firmly in God's knowing everything we humans do. In his famous *Thirteen Principles of the Faith*, he wrote number ten as follows: "I believe with perfect faith that the Blessed Creator knows all the actions of humans, and all their thoughts, as it is written, 'He Who fashions the hearts of them all, Who discerns all their doings'."[4] Maimonides' thirteen principles were enshrined in the well-known hymn, Yigdal, recited in the Friday night prayers.

Despite Maimonides' firm belief in the omniscience of the Supreme Being, he also admitted that resolving the conflict of God's knowledge of our deeds, and our choice to behave in moral or immoral ways, is beyond our comprehension. In the same way that we cannot understand the essence of God, neither can we fathom God's ways.

In Isaiah 55:8, we read "My thoughts are not your thoughts, neither are your ways My ways, says the Lord." Not that different is this Talmudic idea, that "All is in the hand of Heaven except the fear of Heaven."[5]

Some commentators make one additional point. The concept of free will implies that human beings are not predestined to live one's life under the influence of genetics, environment, etc. The Jewish doctrine of "Teshuvah" teaches us that humans are protean, they can rise above their background. They have the freedom to change, grow, improve, become better people and better Jews. This is all implied in "freedom is given…" And "all depends on the majority of one's deeds."

4 Psalms 33:15

5 Tractate Berakhot 33b

Friendship

1:6 – Acquire a companion…

1:7 – Keep far from a bad neighbor, do not associate with a bad person.

"Friendship is one's greatest gift."

Moses ibn Ezra, [1] *Shirat Yisrael*

In the Bible, the friendship between David and Jonathan [2] is well known. When the first King of Israel, Saul, wanted to select a successor, it was naturally his son Jonathan whom he chose. Saul's jealousy of David caused him to expel David from his court [3] and Jonathan demonstrated his steadfast love for his friend David, even risking his life for him more than once. Saul even tried to have David killed, so that his son would have no competition. However, Jonathan was so loyal to his beloved friend David, that he assisted his faithful companion in every way possible. Fearing that Saul's anger toward David would lead to aggression and thus jeopardize the close friendship of the two men, Jonathan exacted an oath from David that would spare Jonathan and his successors. At their last meeting the two close friends entered another covenant which stipulated that David would be king and Jonathan his first minister. [4] When Jonathan was killed with his father and two brothers by the Philistines at Mount Gilboa, [5] David tore his clothing in grief, intoned a dirge, lamenting that, "I grieve for you, my brother Jonathan. You were most dear to me. Your love was wonderful to me, surpassing the love of women."

Several rabbi friends of mine have named their sons David and Jonathan, in the hope that the two children would establish a close, intimate and loving relationship resembling that of biblical David and Jonathan. What wonderful role models they were!

1 Spain, d. 1138
2 I Samuel 18, 20, 23
3 I Samuel 19:1-7
4 I Samuel 23:16-18
5 II Samuel 1:17-27

There is a great emphasis in the Bible on friendship. Besides that of David and Jonathan, there is Ruth and Naomi, and many verses in the Book of Proverbs. For example, "Plans fail for lack of counsel, but with many advisers they succeed". [(6)]

All of us have many acquaintances, but we have few very close friends. I deeply cherish those I have.

A friend is someone with whom we can share our secrets, our faults, and our dreams, and know that no matter what, we will still be accepted and loved.

While it is difficult to admit, in our short lifetime it is not possible to have more than a handful of true friends. The reason, I believe, is that deep friendship requires a great deal of effort, time and energy. In our busy lives, consumed with making a living, caring for our family, cultivating our hobbies and enjoying the highly valued preoccupations in which we are involved, there is precious little time to relate to another human being on a more than superficial level. We can do it only with a precious few. Often it will be friends of long-standing.

My closest friends are people with whom I shared an important early experience. The bonds we create when young are often the strongest, and the loyalties we forge at the earliest stages of life are often the longest lasting. When I think of my closest friends – and there is only a handful – true, deep friends – they are people with whom I shared the experience of high school or summer camp. While I cherish friends made later in life, it is frankly difficult to find the space in our crowded lives to make room for more than those we already have developed.

The Talmud gives good advice for leading a full life. There are two role models who will have great influence on one's life, implies Rabbi Yehoshua ben Perahia. [(7)] "Choose yourself a mentor, and acquire a friend." [(8)] Rabbi Yehoshua believed that a good friend will feel free to give constructive criticism, and will be someone who can be trusted not to reveal confidences. In another oft-quoted passage, the Talmud teaches "Either friendship of death." [(9)]

6 Proverbs 15:22; See also Proverbs 12:26, 13:20, 17:17, 18:24, 22:24-25, 27:17

7 Second century BCE

8 Pirkei Avot 1:6

9 Tractate Taanit 23a

The Hasidic master Rabbi Simhah Bunam [10] seems to have agreed with this idea, when he taught, "It is very necessary for every person to have at least one sincere friend, one true companion. This friend must be so close to us that we are able to tell even that of which we are ashamed."

All agree that maintaining a friendship requires great trust. The English novelist, George Eliot [11] wrote about friendship that it "is the comfort, the inexpressible comfort of feeling safe with a person having neither to weigh thoughts nor measure words, but pouring all right out just as they are, chaff and grain together, certain that a faithful friendly hand will take and sift them, keep what is worth keeping and with a breath of comfort, blow the rest away."

The great medieval collection of moral advice, *Menorat HaMaor*, penned by Rabbi Isaac Aboab [12] lays out a detailed prescription for the cultivation of good friends: "Be first to greet your fellow man. Invite him to your joyous occasions. Call him by complimentary names. Do not give away his secrets; help him when he is in trouble. Look after his interests when he is away. Overlook his shortcomings and forgive him promptly. Criticize him when he has done wrong. Respect him always. Do not deceive him. Do not lie to him. Pray for him and wish him happiness."

Many are the blessings and fruits of close friendships. In the words of General/President Dwight D. Eisenhower, "Friendships have defended more borders than arms and cannon ever have."

Rabbi Abraham Yitzhak Kook, [13] first Chief Rabbi of Eretz Yisrael, wrote this about friendship: "Part of the characteristic of Torah is that it recognizes the need for a social life with friendships, which bring to the world a good life within society. This is particularly rewarding when one's social group consists of good and scholarly people. Separation from other people and extreme asceticism… is a foreign idea to the Torah. For that reason, if one wants to acquire knowledge of Torah, he will succeed specifically by joining together with a group of learners, which shows the gains of avoiding isolation."

---

10 Poland, d. 1827

11 d. 1880

12 14th century, Spain

13 *Land of Israel*, d. 1935

For this reason the method of Torah study in recent times is done in pairs – which is called in "hevruta," or learning with a companion.

Maimonides writes that "people require friends all their lifetime."[(14)]

There is an oft-told story about a *"tzaddik in peltz,"* a so-called righteous person who warms himself with a winter coat, while those around him remain cold. A true tzaddik would be concerned not only with his own welfare, but that of his friends as well.

Some commentators focus on the Hebrew word for "acquire." Namely, it costs a person to make a friend, who must give of oneself, such as warmth, caring, openness, honesty, integrity and trust. Rabbi Abraham J. Twerski quotes the Hasidic leader Rabbi Elimelekh of Lizhensk who recommends "that we have a trusted friend in whom we can confide, and to whom we can reveal all our thoughts as well as our actions."

Rashi has an unusual interpretation on the phrase "acquire a friend." He writes that the Mishnah may be referring to books, which can be great friends. Entering a home of a devoted Jew, one immediately sees a large library of holy Jewish books, which make wonderful friends.

14 *Guide for the Perplexed,* 3:49

God and Human Beings

2:4 – Do His will as if it were yours, so that He may do your will as if it were His. Set aside your will for the sake of His, that He may set aside the will of others before yours.

2:20 – The day is short, the task is great, the laborers are lazy, the reward is much, and the Master insistent.

3:8 – Give Him what is His, for you and yours are His.

3:13 – Anyone who is liked by his fellow human beings is liked by God; anyone who is not like by human beings is not liked by God.

These four sentences of Mishnayot summarize the Weltanschauung of the Jew. To live a God-intoxicated and God-centered life. A life of holiness. A life, as my late beloved teacher, Rabbi Abraham Joshua Heschel, famously wrote, to live a life in radical amazement:

"Get up in the morning and look at the world in a way that takes nothing for granted. Everything is phenomenal; everything is incredible; never treat life casually. To be spiritual is to be amazed ... Awareness of the Divine begins with wonder ... The beginning of our happiness lies in the understanding that life without wonder is not worth living ... What we lack is not a will to believe, but a will to wonder."

Mahzor Vitry taught in the eleventh century that a Jew must "strive to do the will of God, with a perfect heart and a willing soul, and cancel out your will, even if obeying the will of God includes suffering."

The aim of all life is to emulate God's holiness. Living a holy life means pursuing a set of values that include loving our neighbor, protecting the stranger, caring for the poor, the hungry, and the widow.[1]

Maimonides taught, "When the Torah says 'be holy,' it means exactly the same as if it said, 'fulfill My commandments'"[2]

It becomes clear when studying the Jewish sources on the subject of holiness that living a holy life equals living a moral life.

1 *Cf.* Isaiah 58:5-8

2 *Sefer HaMitzvot*

The Hellenistic Jewish philosopher, Philo, [3] wrote that "Holiness toward God and justice toward men usually go together."

The Talmud teaches that one attains holiness by modeling one's life on the attributes of God: "As God is merciful, so be you merciful; as God is gracious, be you gracious." [4]

The well-known British sage, Rabbi Louis Jacobs, [5] explains holiness in practical, modern terms. "In life today, for example, how many drinks a man should have in one evening, how much time he should spend watching television, which kind of films he should see, which type of books he should read, and what stand he should take on the moral issues of the day – all such matters cannot belong to Torah legislation. But that a man's religion compels him to put such questions to himself is basic to a sound religious outlook on life and it is the asking of the questions and the sincere attempt to answer them in the spirit of Judaism that is meant by the command to be holy." [6]

One of the wisest comments on living a holy life, commensurate with living in God's presence, is that of Dag Hammarskjold, [7] the Swedish diplomat and author, who was the second Secretary-General of the United Nations, in his book, *Markings*: "In our era, the road to holiness necessarily passes through the world of action."

Often we ask the question, "Who is a good Jew?" My late beloved teacher, Rabbi Louis Finkelstein [8] gave his answer to this question: "A good Jew is a Jew who is always trying to become a better Jew." I frequently taught that answer to my students and my congregants. Our present Mishnah asks this question in this form: How best can we serve God? In the Talmud we find this reply: [9]

Abaye said: "As it was taught in a baraita that it is stated: 'And you shall love the Lord your God,' [10] which means that you shall make the name of Heaven beloved. How should one do so? One

3 Alexandria, Egypt, d. 50 CE
4 Tractate Shabbat 133b
5 d. 2006
6 *The Jewish Religion*, p. 246
7 d. 1961
8 New York, d. 1991
9 Tractate Yoma 86a
10 Deuteronomy 6:5

should do so in that he should read Torah, and learn Mishna, and serve Torah scholars, and he should be pleasant with people in his business transactions.

"What do people say about such a person? Fortunate is his father who taught him Torah, fortunate is his teacher who taught him Torah, woe to the people who have not studied Torah. So-and-so, who taught him Torah, see how pleasant are his ways, how proper are his deeds. The verse states about him and others like him: 'You are My servant, Israel, in whom I will be glorified.'" [11]

But one who reads Torah, and learns Mishnah, and serves Torah scholars, but his business practices are not done faithfully, and he does not speak pleasantly with other people, what do people say about him? Woe to so-and-so who studied Torah, woe to his father who taught him Torah, woe to his teacher who taught him Torah. So-and-so who studied Torah, see how destructive are his deeds, and how ugly are his ways.

Several commentators took special note of 3:8, "Give Him what is His, for you and yours are His" with the understanding that when we generously give of ourselves, whether to charity, or to any worthy causes, monetarily or not, that it all comes from God – and we make contributions because in essence what we give are gifts to us from God. It is therefore Jewish custom to thank God before many things we do. We recite brakhot (blessings) before eating food, because the source of all sustenance is God. "The earth is the Lord's and all that it holds, the world and its inhabitants." [12] With that in mind, all charity which we donate, all sustenance which we receive, it is important for a spiritual person to acknowledge the Source, God Almighty. Furthermore, as the great Italian rabbi of the fifteenth century, Ovadiah of Bartenura, wrote, "We should be as generous with our giving to others in need as we are to ourselves in fulfilling our own needs."

Regarding 2:4, "Set aside your will for the sake of His." Rashi quotes rabbinic sources that a person should not say, "I loathe pork," but instead, "I very much like pork, but my heavenly Father has forbidden me to eat it." [13]

---

11 Isaiah 49:3

12 Psalms 24:1

13 On Leviticus 20:26, from Sifra, Kedoshim, Chapter 12:23

On that same Mishnah, on the same phrase, our Sages taught that "One who seeks to purify oneself will be helped by God to achieve the goal." [14] In other words, when we make an attempt to set aside our own desires in favor of God's, we are assisted by the Almighty Himself.

Regarding 3:13, "Anyone who is liked by his fellow human beings is liked by God; anyone who is not liked by human beings is not liked by God", to me this means that we should love our fellow human beings because they are made in the image of God. We should love others because they are all God's children.

14 Tractate Shabbat 104a

History

1:1 – Moses received Torah at Sinai and handed it on to Yehoshua. Yehoshua to the elders. The elders to the prophets, and the prophets handed it on to the men of the Great Assembly. They said ...

There are several crucial lessons derived from this first Mishnah in Pirkei Avot. First, since it is the opening and introductory statement, it sets the tone for the remainder of the tractate. Second, what this opening statement tells us is that everything starts with the receiving of Torah from Sinai by Moses Rabbenu. Third, the statement sends a clear message about all the words that follow; namely, that though it starts at Sinai, it does not end there. "Everything that any future scholar teaches ... was already said to Moses at Sinai." (1)

The importance of this statement in the Jerusalem Talmud cannot be overestimated. What the Sages are declaring is that while Torah is from Sinai, Jewish tradition has continued to develop in an authentic, unbroken chain of tradition from that time, three thousand years ago, to the present. Each generation, each new group of scholars, expanded the Torah given to Moses and added explanation after explanation.

The above teaching is adumbrated in this astounding, imaginary conversation related in the Talmud: (2) "When Moses ascended to the heavens, he found the Holy One sitting and attaching crowns to the letters.

He said before Him, "Master of the Universe! Who is restraining your hand?"

He said to him, "There is one man who will exist after several generations, and Akiva the son of Yosef is his name, who will in the future expound on every crown and crown piles and piles of laws."

He said before Him, "Master of the Universe! Show him to me."

He said to him, "Turn backwards."

He went and sat at the end of eight rows [of students in Rabbi Akiva's Beit Midrash [academy], and he did not know what they

1 Jerusalem Talmud Hagigah 1:8

2 Tractate Menahot 29b

were talking about. He got upset. When Rabbi Akiva got to another topic, his students said to him, "Our teacher, from where do you learn this?"

He said to them, "It is a law [that was taught] to Moses at Sinai." His mind was set at ease.

The rabbis were intent on ascribing Divine authority to this tractate, even though it differed from much of the rest of the Talmud.

Bartenura commented on the opening Mishnah in Avot as follows: "I say: Since this tractate is not founded on the exegesis of commandments from among the Torah's commandments, like the rest of the tractates which are in the Mishna, but is rather wholly morals and principles, and whereas the sages of the (other) nations of the world have also composed books according to the fabrication of their hearts, concerning moral paths, how a person should behave with his fellow. Therefore, in this tractate the *Tanna* [rabbinic Sage of the Mishnah] began, 'Moses received Torah from Sinai,' to tell you that the principles and morals which are in this tractate were not fabricated by the hearts of the Mishna's Sages; rather, they too were stated at Sinai."

The Netziv, Naftali Tzvi Berlin, (3) explains the transition from the traditionalist to the innovative midrashic approach to the Torah as parallel to the transition from the first tablets at Sinai written by God to the second ones written by Moses:

"In the first tablets there was no gift of *Hidush* [change] at all but Torah was whatever Moses heard with its basis in the Written Torah. Moses did not know how to make his own *Hidush* except to think analogically but without creative pilpul. But in the second tablets the power of *Hidush* was granted to innovate new halakhot in every generation. That is the meaning of the Rabbinic phrase that 'everything that a veteran student of Torah will in the future innovate is already given at Sinai.' The power to innovate, not the content, is given. (4)

"The reason God ordered Moses to carve the second tablets was not because they were not worthy of a Divine act, but to teach that the ever-renewing power of halakhah given in the second tablets

3 Russia, d. 1893

4 *Ha'amek Davar*, Deuteronomy 4:14

involves the active participation of the labor of human beings with Divine aid, just as the second tablets were carved by Moses and the writing was by God."[5]

It seems clear that the Sages were making another statement, in addition to the above. That is, to disprove the claim of the Sadducees who argued that the rabbis of the Talmud (the Pharisees) were deviating from the Torah; that the far-reaching interpretations of the Talmudic rabbis had Divine approval. Furthermore, they may also have been arguing that those who followed Paul, and who held that the New Testament had replaced the authority of the Torah (the "Old Testament") were also in error.

5 *Ha'amek Davar,* Exodus 34:1

Humans and Their Neighbors

It should not surprise us that some of the themes embedded in this treatise on Jewish ethics and human behavior, have the same idea expanded to be included in several of the Mishnayot in several chapters in the tractate of Pirkei Avot. We shall take each one and comment on them individually.

2:16 – The evil eye, the evil impulse [yetzer hara], and hatred of humankind drive a person out of the world.

An evil eye implies qualities of greed and envy, not the moral virtues encouraged by the Sages. One possessing these evil qualities defeats the purpose of creation, as seen by Jewish tradition.

Jewish tradition tells us that each person has a good inclination (*yetzer hatov*) and an evil inclination (*yetzer hara*). In a popular legend of unknown origin there is a story of two wolves. In the story a grandfather tells his grandson that there are two wolves fighting within each person. When the grandson asks which wolf wins, the grandfather replies: whichever one he chooses to feed.

Commenting on the biblical verse to "love God with all your heart," [(1)] the Sages teach that the word for "your heart" (*l'vav'kha*) has two Hebrew letters "*bet*" – which implies that we have a good inclination and an evil inclination in our heart, and that we should love God with both of them. In other words, use the *yetzer hara* for good purposes. [(2)] "Make your earthly passions and commonplace wants influential in your service to God, in order that there is no place in your heart divided against God. [(3)]

"Hatred of humankind...." This denunciation of misanthropy reflects the biblical command, "You shall not hate your kinsfolk

1 Deuteronomy 6:5
2 Berakhot 54a
3 Midrash, Sifre 73a, Tractate Berakhot 61b

in your heart". [4] However, the Mishnah goes farther than just your "kinsfolk."

Not only is hatred bad, but causeless hatred is even worse. It was the reason for the destruction of the Bet Mikdash (the holy Temple in Jerusalem), and ruins the relationship between husband and wife, and produces children to be born prematurely. [5]

Rabbi Abraham Yitzhak Kook famously taught that instead of causeless hatred (*sin'at hinam*), we should engage in causeless love (*ahavat hinam*).

In her 1979 acceptance speech for the Nobel Peace Prize, Mother Theresa summarized well this Mishnah:

> It is not enough for us to say: "I love God, but I do not love my neighbor." [In the New Testament, (I John 4:20) it is written] How can you love God whom you do not see, if you do not love your neighbor whom you see, whom you touch, with whom you live?

"Humankind"

The Mishnah uses this word, humankind (Hebrew *ha-b'riyot*) implying hatred of all people, not just Jews, drives one out of the world.

"Drive a person out of the world"

Such evil qualities will shorten one's life (Maimonides), or cut one off from society.

4:3 – Despise no one and disdain nothing, for there is no one who does not have his hour…

Shaming God's creatures is equal to shaming God. [6]

The Sages stressed the democratic nature of humanity. We are all creatures of God, all created "*b'tzelem Elohim*" (in the image

4 Leviticus 19:17

5 Tractates Gittin 55b and Shabbat 32b

6 Tractate Bava Metzia 58b, Midrash Genesis Rabbah 24:7

of God). The Talmud stresses human equality in this remarkable passage: [(7)]

> The Sages in Yavne were wont to say: I who learn Torah am God's creature and my counterpart who engages in other labor is God's creature. My work is in the city and his work is in the field. I rise early for my work and he rises early for his work. And just as he does not presume to perform my work, so I do not presume to perform his work. Lest you say: I engage in Torah study a lot, while he only engages in Torah study a little, so I am better than he, it has already been taught: One who brings a substantial sacrifice and one who brings a meager sacrifice have equal merit, as long as he directs his heart towards Heaven.

One commentator reminds us that no one is without potential, and thus no one should be disdained or scorned, since, as the Sages taught, [(8)] "Even the empty-heads are filled with mitzvot as a pomegranate is filled with seeds."

An interesting twist on this Mishnah is given by a slight change in translation. By translating the Hebrew *"l'khol adam,"* (despise no one) as "the entire person," the comment suggests that no one should be despised because of a single fault. We all have at least one fault and no one should disdain us in toto for that one blemish.

"Disdain nothing" – This short phrase is a key part of the modern environmental movement, and has strong roots in Jewish tradition. Rabbi Yitzhak Luria (the "Arizal") of sixteenth century Safed, the lion of the Kabbalah, would not kill an insect, which, as he taught, has a purpose in the scheme of the universe, as do all of God's creatures. Many Sages followed his example, such as Rabbi Abraham Yitzhak Kook, who would not pluck a flower or kill an insect.

If such scholars would honor the tiniest, insignificant creatures made by God, how much more so should we respect every human made in God's image. As the Maharal [(9)] taught: Every person plays a role in the grand scheme of creation, without which the world is

7 Tractate Berakhot 17a

8 Tractate Hagigah 27a

9 Yehudah Lowe of Prague, d. 1609

incomplete.

"For there is no one who does not have his hour..."

The Midrash relates the story of Duklitinus, a shepherd of pigs near Tiberius, who was treated poorly by Jewish children. He later became king and wanted revenge. The rabbis approached him: "Why should we receive punishment for the past? The one who was mistreated was Duklitinus, a shepherd of pigs, not Duklitinus the king." He forgave them and warned them to be more careful in the future. [10]

The wealth of commentaries on Pirkei Avot brings many novel interpretations. One commentator proposes that "there is no one who does not have his hour" can mean that everyone and everything has limitless possibilities. Who would have dreamed a few centuries ago that in the modern age there would be such inventions as airplanes, computers, and the myriad medical discoveries that are available today?

"Who does not have his hour..." may hint at the potential of every human being to recreate oneself in an instant. The traditional Jewish doctrine of Teshuvah implies that at any moment, a person can transform her/himself into a better person. There are innumerable people in history who have done just that. The famed Rabbi Akiba is one startling example. At age forty he transformed himself from an uneducated shepherd to the greatest scholar of his generation. [11]

Winston Churchill was reviled by the British public and by his own party, and later was the first British Prime Minister to win the Nobel Prize in Literature and is considered one of the great figures of modern history.

4:15 – Let your student's honor be as precious to you as your own; let your colleague's honor be like the reverence due to your teacher; and let the reverence you have for your teacher be like the reverence due to Heaven.

---

10 Genesis Rabbah 63:8, Jerusalem Talmud Tractate Terumot 8:4

11 *Avot d'Rabbi Natan* A6

Rabbi Yitzhak Abarbanel, a Portuguese scholar [12] points out that this Mishnah deals with three categories in the learning process: those who are inferior (students), those who are equals (colleagues), and those who are superior (teachers).

This Mishnah affirms another similar teaching: "Much have I learned from my teachers, and from my colleagues, but most from my students." [13]

Maimonides taught: "One must take extreme care with one's students, since they give him pleasure in this world and in the World to Come." [14]

The distinguished rabbi and psychiatrist, Abraham J. Twerski wisely advises: "This verse of the Mishnah should be written in bright, flashing neon lights and displayed in every school. It is possible that a teacher may humiliate a student in front of the class, either by applying discipline inappropriately or by commenting something like, 'That is a stupid question.' A single remark of this type may leave its mark on a student for life."

Respecting colleagues differing opinions was expected among ancient Sages, as reflected in this Talmudic teaching: "Both these opinions and these opinions are the words of the living God." [15]

An astounding comment in Tractate Yevamot (14b) describes the camaraderie among students of the School of Shammai and the School of Hillel, who continually disagreed. Bet Shammai [the School of Shammai, i.e., his students] did not refrain from marrying women from Bet Hillel [the School of Hillel], nor did Bet Hillel refrain from marrying women from Bet Shammai. This serves to teach you that they practiced love and friendship between them, to fulfill that which is stated: "Love truth and peace." [16]

In another Talmudic passage we find that the scholars of Babylonia would rise for each other and would tear their clothes in mourning when a colleague died. [17]

Regarding honoring teachers, there are many examples in our

12 d. 1508
13 Tractate Taanit 7a
14 Hilkhot Talmud Torah 5:12
15 Tractate Eruvin 13b
16 Zechariah 8:19
17 Tractate Bava Metzia 33a

tradition. In the Torah, Aaron refers to his younger brother, Moses, as "my master".[18] In rabbinic times, Rabbi Meir famously honored his teacher, Rabbi Elisha ben Avuyah (known as "*aher*" (the "other") despite his heretical views, while other scholars deserted him.

4:20 – Be first in greeting everyone. Be a tail to lions rather than a head to foxes.

Rabbi Moses Hayyim Luzzatto[19] was one of the great kabbalists and ethicists of his time. In his introduction to his famous ethical work, *The Path of the Just,* he writes that most of what his book contains is not anything we do not know already. His book is not filled with insights and novelties; it is common sense knowledge we are all familiar with. But somehow, that which is so simple and obvious to us all, perhaps because it is so obvious, is typically neglected by many people. A suggestion to be the first to greet others seems obvious, yet is not always carried out.

There are many ways to parse this Mishnah. One obvious way is that everyone deserves a warm greeting, Jew or gentile, and especially if it is a person with whom you are in a dispute. Often by being the first to initiate a greeting, it may put the opponent off balance, and cause her/him to respond in a friendly manner – and perhaps even resolve the issue. As the Psalmist teaches, "Seek peace and pursue it." Not only should we always want to have peaceful relations with others, we must often chase after a friendly relationship.

Professor Ron Wolfson has written a very influential book, appropriately titled *Relational Judaism* in which he argues that synagogues can be transformed by more warmth and welcoming approaches. The promotion for the book describes its purpose in these words: "This inspiring handbook both establishes a sound foundation for why a deep hospitality is crucial for the survival of today's spiritual communities, and dives into the practical hands-on of turning your congregation into a place of invitation and openness." Sounds to me like the fulfillment of our Mishnah.

18 Numbers 12:11
19 Early 18th century Italy

In the early morning prayers (Shaharit) we find this introductory passage from the Mishnah: "These are things for which one enjoys the fruits in this world while the principal remains for her/him in the world to come … bringing peace between a person and her/his neighbor." [20]

Aaron is known for exactly this kind of positive peace seeking. In *Avot d'Rabbi Natan* (12:3) we learn: When Aaron would see two people quarreling, he would go to each one of them without the knowledge of his fellow and say to him, "Behold how your fellow is regretting and afflicting himself that he sinned against you; and he told me that I should come to you so that you will forgive him." And as a result of this, when they bumped into each other, they would kiss each other. And how would he bring people closer to the Torah? When he would know about someone who has committed a sin, he would befriend him and show him a friendly demeanor; and that man would be embarrassed and say [to himself], "If that righteous man would know my evil deeds, how much would he distance himself from me?" And as a result of this, [that man] would change for the better. And this is what the prophet testifies about [Aaron], "In peace and in straightness did he walk with Me and he brought back many from sinning." [21]

Some commentators view this as a warning to Jews who live in a non-Jewish environment, and suggest that by being friendly and welcoming to others, their status in the community will be more secure.

"Be a tail to lions rather than a head to foxes."

Lions are known for their strength, while foxes are known for their craftiness. In the realm of the spirit, it is always better to be among people who are spiritually stronger than you than among those who are spiritually less than you. Rashi comments that it is better to be a humble follower of righteous people than the leader of people who are ordinary individuals.

Maimonides explains the Talmudic passage: When a judge was promoted from the bet din of 23 judges to the higher court of 71 judges, he would go from being the head of the smaller court to

20 Tractate Peah 1:1

21 Malachi 2

being the "tail" of the higher bet din. [22] If he complained about going from the "head" to the "tail," he was told, "In matters of holiness we ascend, we do not descend. [23] Such a 'descent' is in fact an "ascent." Before you were a head to foxes, but now you are a tail to lions."

4:23 – Do not try to placate your friend in his hour of anger. Do not try to comfort him while his dead lies before him … Do not try to see him in his hour of disgrace.

It is a constant source of amazement to me how often I find that the psychological insights of our ancient Sages anticipate so many wise principles of good mental health. The advice in this Mishnah bears out that view. Many commentators throughout the ages share the following summary of this Mishnah. Maimonides, for example, said to his son, Abraham, "Think about what you are going to say before you say it." In other words, timing is everything. The biblical book of Ecclesiastes taught long before, "There is a time for everything" (3:1). In all cases, the intent may be worthy, but at the wrong time it may very well be harmful.

Maimonides, in his commentary on Avot, teaches that one should offer advice only when it will be effective.

Modern psychology teaches that it is important to express our emotions, or they become dangerously bottled up with negative repercussions later in life. Anger, grief and shame are a natural and useful part of our nature. Whoever tries to interrupt this natural process with words of appeasement, comfort or support, prematurely, does no good. More likely they are covering up their own discomfort rather than helping a friend. Negative feelings, such as anger, grief and shame can be cathartic and should be processed in a natural fashion. Often psychotherapy may be required. Effective support from a friend has its time, which is not before the listener is ready. As the Talmud teaches, "Just as it is a mitzvah for a person to say that which will be heeded, so is it a mitzvah for a person not to say that which will not be heeded." [24]

22 Tractate Sanhedrin 37a
23 Tractate Berakhot 28a
24 Tractate Yevamot 65b

At a premature time, the appeasement, comfort and support in these cases will surely not only not be heeded, but will probably exacerbate the situation. More than likely, such comments will likely add insult to injury.

The friends of Job are a good example of poor timing, when intended comfort can possibly become criticism or mockery.

Bartenura gives an example from God Himself. When the Bet Mikdash was burned by the Romans, God was crying, and the angels tried to offer God comfort. God replied: Do not hasten to comfort me. We can suppose that even God has a need to vent Divine emotions.

Regarding trying to help an angry person, Rashi teaches that the person will not only not be appeased, more likely she/he will grow more angry. Rabbi Berel Wein shares personal experiences that I am many other colleagues can identify with: "I have often been at houses of mourning where those who are attempting to comfort the mourners mouth banalities and statements that actually hurt the already grief-stricken mourners. When a wound is still open, one must be very careful as to what type of balm to place upon it."

Judgment

1:6 – Give everyone the benefit of the doubt.

Once again, a short and seemingly simple phrase packs a wallop of deep, strong advice. Far too often we accuse others of failures, sins, mistakes, missteps, with little or no basis. This is true in everyday life, as well as in the world of politics. What this Mishnah is telling us is not to assume the worst of people, but, on the contrary, always attempt to discover valid reasons for seemingly negative behavior. Such negative assumptions destroy the atmosphere of trust and safety which must prevail to maintain a healthy society.

The Talmud teaches: "One who judges others favorably will in turn be judged favorably in heaven." [1]

The most dramatic example of a person who gave others the benefit of the doubt is the famous Hasidic master, Rabbi Levi Yitzhak of Berdichev. [2] The following story illustrates the lesson:

It happened that Rabbi Levi Yitzhak of Berdichev went strolling in the city on the fast day of Tishah B'Av.

He noticed a Jew eating and drinking publicly. He approached him and said: My son, surely you forgot that today is Tishah B'Av.

No, our master, I know that today is Tishah B'Av.

Therefore, continued Rabbi Levi Yitzhak, you must not know that on Tishah B'Av, it is forbidden to eat and drink.

No, our master, said the man, firm in his opinion, I know that today is a fast day.

I am certain, said Rabbi Levi Yitzhak, validating the man's opinion, that you are not well, and observing a fast would endanger your health.

No, our master, he smiled, I am very healthy, and may all Jews be so healthy.

Rabbi Levi Yitzhak lifted his eyes to heaven and said: Master of the universe, look down from heaven and see what a wonderful, holy people are Your Jewish people. Three times I gave him an

1 Tractate Shabbat 127b

2 Poland, d. 1809

opportunity to lie, and still he tells the truth! [3]

Does that mean that we must never upbraid or criticize anyone? Does not the Torah admonish: "You shall surely rebuke your neighbor"? [4] The Torah's command does not contradict our Mishnah. There is a proper time for giving chastisement, when one is certain that our neighbor can be helped by constructive criticism. And there is a proper time to give one the benefit of a doubt.

Another great Hasidic master, the Baal Shem Tov, the founder of Hasidism in the eighteenth century, taught that the world is a mirror of ourselves. Since humans are not likely to acknowledge their own faults in character, God allows us to see them in other people. Thus, if we see a failure or defect in someone else, we should realize that it may be our own reflection that we see, and that such a fault is really ours. This follows the Talmudic dictum, "Whoever disqualifies others, that is a sign that he himself is flawed." [5] Psychologists today call this "projection." Whatever fault is within us, we project on to another.

The literal translation of the Hebrew in this Mishnah, is "Judge everyone in the scale of merit." Picture a scale with two pans, on the left is a "scale of merit," and on the right "a scale of guilt." Each person's deeds are weighed on such a scale. And each deed we perform can tip the scale in either direction. So, advises the Mishnah, always judge a person as if the scale is tipped towards the left side, "the scale of merit." The Talmud teaches: A person should view oneself as though he were exactly half-liable and half-innocent. [6] In other words, one should act as though the plates of the scale are balanced, so that if he/she performs one mitzvah he/she is fortunate, as he/she tilts the balance to the scale of merit. If one transgresses one prohibition, woe to him/her, as he/she tilts the balance to the scale of guilt, as it is stated: "But one sin destroys much good", which means that due to one sin that a person transgresses he/she squanders much good. [7]

---

3 From *Loving and Beloved: Stories of Rabbi Levi Yitzhak of Berdichev*, Simcha Raz, translated by Dov Peretz Elkins

4 Leviticus 19:17

5 Tractate Kiddushin 70b

6 Tractate Kiddushin 40b

7 Ecclesiastes 9:18

The Talmud gives this example of the advice in our Mishnah: "If you saw a Torah scholar transgress a prohibition at night, do not think badly of him during the day; perhaps he has repented in the meantime." [8] Rashi comments on this Mishnah that a person who gives others the benefit of the doubt will himself be given the same favorable judgment in the Heavenly court.

Rabbi Shimshon Raphael Hirsch [9] comments, "It should be our endeavor to keep the best possible opinion of all people, and even in cases where conduct seems of dubious character, we should be as charitable as we can in our judgment."

An interesting footnote to this Mishnah relates to its author, Rabbi Yehoshua ben Perahya. The Talmud relates that this second century rabbi was the teacher of Jesus. Rabbi Yehoshua rejected his student for certain bad conduct, and later the teacher regretted his treatment of Jesus, and thus this teaching of giving everyone the benefit of a doubt. Rabbi Benny Lau suggests that this Mishnah is the result of Rabbi Yehoshua's regret, since Jesus went on to be the central figure of Christianity. [10]

1:9 – Examine the witnesses thoroughly, and be careful in your words, lest through them they learn how to lie.

Jewish law, from the Torah forward, has had a strong emphasis on fairness and equal justice for all. "You shall do no unrighteousness in judgment: do not favor the poor or show deference to the rich. Judge your kinsman in fairness". [11]

Fair laws and a just court system have always been considered in Jewish tradition as signs of an enlightened society. While there are 613 commandments in the Torah that apply to Jews, there are seven for which all humans are responsible – the "Seven Commandments of the Descendants of Noah" (all humankind). One of these laws is to establish courts of justice. In important cases, the Torah demands that the elders "examine and inquire and interrogate thoroughly." [12]

8 Tractate Berakhot 19a

9 Frankfurt, Germany, d. 1888

10 From Rabbi Irving Greenberg, *Sage Advice*

11 Leviticus 19:15

12 Deuteronomy 13:15

"The examination of witnesses in Jewish Law was very different from what obtained in Egypt, Rome and Athens, where torture was the order of the day. The fourth Book of Maccabees (8:13) gives a list of the horrible instruments of torture used to extract evidence from witnesses – wheels, joint screws, dislocators, rocks and bone crushers, catapults, cauldrons, braziers, thumb screws, iron claws, wedges and branding irons. Judaism, to its eternal glory, never practiced torture." [(13)]

"Moses promulgated laws that replaced the arbitrary power of a pharaoh or king with just rules that applied to everyone equally. This was 700 years before the Athenian leader Pericles declared proudly that Athens was governed by equal justice." [(14)] The same author points out that the author of this Mishnah, Shimon ben Shetah established the first systematic cross-examination of witnesses, which became a model for Roman law and then later for European jurisprudence.

While this commentary does not, in general, focus on the biographical background of the Talmudic Sages, on occasion the events of an author's life bear important information on their advice. In the case of Shimon ben Shetah, author of this Mishnah, some background information is crucial. One of my favorite stories in the Talmud is one in which this Sage is the "hero."

His fairness is illustrated by the following narrative: He lived in humble circumstances, supporting himself and his family by conducting a small business in linen goods. Once his pupils presented him with a donkey which they had purchased from a gentile merchant. Using the legal formula prescribed by the Talmud, they said, "When we pay you, this donkey and everything on it is ours." After receiving the gift, the rabbi removed the saddle and discovered an expensive gem. The students happily told their master that he might now stop toiling since the proceeds from the jewel would make him wealthy – the legal formula of the sale meant that the jewel was now his property. Shimon ben Shetah, however, replied that even though the letter of the law said they were right, it was clear that the seller had no intention of selling the jewel along with the animal. Shimon returned the gem to the

13 Shlomo P. Toperoff, *Avot*, p. 46
14 William Berkson, *Pirke Avot*, p. 31

merchant, who exclaimed, "Praised be the God of Shimon ben Shetah!" That statement by a gentile was more precious to Rabbi Shimon than all the world's riches. (15)

This story illustrates the author's passion for honesty. Another Talmudic story about him also testifies to his concern for justice. His son was condemned to death and executed on a groundless charge. (16) Obviously the rabbi was concerned that equal and fair justice be applied in all cases.

"Lest through them they learn how to lie."

The final words of this Mishnah may also apply to parents and how they raise their children. Often parents tell "white lies" to, or in front of, their children, not realizing what a negative influence they are having. For example, on entering a movie theater, or other place of entertainment, a parent may advise the child to pretend she/he is below a certain age in order to get a child's discount. The child will then learn that it is acceptable to lie to gain favors.

4:10 – Do not act as a judge alone, for none may judge alone except the One. Do not say "Accept my view;" for they are permitted, not you.

This Mishnah, as many in Pirkei Avot, has multiple layers of meaning. Its primary intention is to advise judges, but many commentators suggest that it has clear implications for everyone. We all make judgments, and judgment calls.

By stating that "none may judge alone except One," the teaching reminds us that only God makes judgments alone. We mortals need to rely on the advice of friends and colleagues. "God stands in the Divine assembly; among the Divine beings God pronounces judgment." (17)

Every judge and every individual should recognize her/his limits. As mortals, our judgments are finite, and often have serious consequences. The more serious the judgment, the more important it is to consult others before making a decision. When a judge pronounces a death sentence, he/she should realize that the decision

15 Jerusalem Talmud, Bava Metzia 2:5, Midrash Deuteronomy Rabbah 3:5

16 Jerusalem Talmud Sanhedrin 6:3

17 Psalms 82:1

affects not only the defendant, but also the unborn children who would have emerged had the person been given the chance to remain alive.

There's an old saying that bears out this idea: "If one person tells you you're a horse, they are crazy. If three people tell you you're a horse, there's conspiracy afoot. If ten people tell you you're a horse, it's time to buy a saddle." Truth is not always in large numbers, but large number of opinions should be taken seriously. One cannot laugh them off.

The Talmud relates that when Rav Huna was considering an important decision, he would gather ten Sages from the study hall to rule together with him, so that if an error was made the responsibility would not be his alone. "So that I will receive only a small splinter from the beam."[18]

In Jewish literature, the word for justice (*mishpat*) is frequently coupled with the word for mercy *(hesed*, or *rahamim*). Sound judgment when combined with gentleness, mercy, and compassion, is more likely to be fair and impartial.

Since we all make judgments on a regular basis in our lives, it is incumbent upon every human being to act with humility. Telling others "accept my view," or, as arrogant people express this thought, "my way or the highway," is uncalled for, and unproductive. The Talmud teaches that "Whoever walks with a pompous mindset, it is as though he/she pushes away the Divine Presence."[19]

As a writer, I never submit a manuscript to a publisher without first having several friends and colleagues render feedback. The wise Hasidic master, Rabbi Menahem Mendel of Kotzk[20] taught that "Not everything that one thinks is fit to say; not everything that one says is fit to write; not everything that one writes is fit to publish." Humility among authors is good advice for all of us who make judgments on a daily basis.

18 Tractate Sanhedrin 7b

19 Tractate Berakhot 43b

20 Poland, d. 1859

Kiruv (Jewish Outreach)

1:12 – Be among the disciples of Aaron, loving peace and pursuing peace, loving people and drawing them close to the Torah.

This Mishnah is one of the most well-known and oft-quoted sentences in Pirkei Avot. It carries a heavy load of meaning, altruism and universalism. The reason is not hard to find. Aaron is one of the most beloved personalities in the Torah. His inspiring and momentous ideals are championed by people of good will throughout the world.

Although responsible for the creation of the Golden Calf, his action to appease the impatient throng waiting for his younger brother, Moses, to descend Mount Sinai, is seen by many commentators as a saving and helpful deed. It seems that Aaron's instinct for conciliation is his primary modus operandum.

The legends spun around him in rabbinic literature abound, so much so that the rabbis lift up the verse in the prophet Malakhi (2:6) in which God praises Aaron to the sky: "Proper rulings were in his mouth, and nothing perverse was on his lips; he walked with Me in complete loyalty, and held the many back from iniquity."

Rabbi Gordon Tucker makes an astute observation on the original Hebrew text: "The word *m'karvan* (drawing them close) has the very same root letters as the Hebrew word for sacrifice, *korban*. The Aaron we thought we knew was the one who 'brought offerings close' to the altar, while the rest of the community – the non-priests – were warned not to come close to the off-limits holy space. The Aaron we are now urged to emulate is one who does not live and work within walls that keep the unauthorized out, but rather touches people everywhere in an effort to bring them closer to the source of holiness – which is not the altar, but rather a life lived in Torah."[(1)]

Among the legends spun around Aaron, as we mentioned above, are these, from *Avot d'Rabbi Natan*:

The story is told that Aaron would be walking along and, upon encountering a wicked person, would greet that person with peace. Later, when the same person was on his way to worship [idolatry],

1 *Pirkei Avot Lev Shalem*

he said: Woe unto me! How can I look Aaron in the eye without being ashamed before him, for he greeted me with peace!? And so, the person in the end refrained from idolatrous worship.

In another tale two people had a quarrel, and Aaron went and sat with one of them and said, "My son, see what your friend is doing, for he is in a state of emotional turmoil, rending his garments and, all choked up, saying: How can I look my friend in the eye? I am ashamed before him, for it was I who did wrong."

He would sit with him until he removed all jealousy from his heart. Afterwards he would go to his friend and say to him, "My son, see what your friend is doing. For he is in a state of emotional turmoil, rending his garments and, all choked up, saying: How can I look my friend in the eye? I am ashamed before him, for it was I who did wrong to him." He would sit there until he removed all jealousy from his heart. When the two met, they embraced and kissed each other. Therefore, it is written, "All the house of Israel bewailed Aaron thirty days." [2]

"Loving peace and pursuing peace."

Commentators ask about the difference between "loving peace" and "pursuing peace." Maharal explains that "loving peace" relates to preventing new arguments from occurring, while "pursuing peace" relates to existing disputes.

Notice that the Mishnah does not say that Aaron loved Jews, but it uses the Hebrew word *beriyot,* which means "creatures," and implies all living creatures, everything created by God.

Jewish tradition emphasized respect for gentiles in many passages. "We greet and inquire after the welfare of gentiles because of ways of peace." [3]

"We salute gentiles the same way we salute Jews, 'peace unto you'. [4]

We support the poor of the gentiles with the poor of Jews.

We visit the sick of the gentiles with the sick of Jews.

We bury the dead of the gentiles as we bury the dead of Jews because of the ways of peace." [5]

---

2 Num. 20:29

3 Mishnah Sheviit 4:3

4 Jerusalem Talmud Tractate Sheviit 4:35b

5 Gittin 61a

Tamar Elad-Appelbaum wisely points to another Hebrew language lesson, that the Hebrew word for responsibility, "*aharayut*," has within it the Hebrew word for "other – *aheir*," ... "thus suggesting that responsible people are those deeply imbued with a sense of obligation toward others ... and the recognition that others' instances of distress and discomfort are, in some way, their own. The internal acceptance of responsibility manifests itself externally in encounters with others, and signals an individual's readiness to draw near to the Torah and its value. The love of human beings itself draws people close to the love of Torah". [(6)]

Notice that the Mishnah states first that Aaron loves humanity, and only then does he, is he able to, bring them close to Torah and Torah values. Thus, people will listen to you if they know that you care for them. A good lesson for all who have something to teach.

---

6 *Pirkei Avot Lev Shalem*

Learning and Teaching

1:4 – Let your house be a meeting place for Sages. Sit in the dust at their feet, and with thirst, drink in their words.

Since Torah and Torah-knowledge is the basis of a vital and vibrant Jewish life, it is not surprising that many of the choice statements in Avot are based around the importance of, the need for, ways to achieve Torah wisdom and Torah values. Clearly the most frequently discussed topic through Avot is study of Torah.

What is the most important locus for learning and absorbing Torah knowledge and Torah values? Is it the school, the synagogue, or the home? This Mishnah hits the nail on the head: it's the home, hands down.

Rabbi Shlomo P. Toperoff wisely writes, [1] "We visit the Synagogue, but we live in the home. The greater number of mitzvot one practices is in the home. The home is a miniature Temple and sanctuary."

Knowledge of Torah is fundamental to living a Jewish life. In Avot we find that it is one of the three pillars upon which the world stands: on the Torah on Divine worship, and on deeds of kindness. [2]

What is the best way to learn Torah? From books? Not so, implies this Mishnah. The most effective way to learn and practice Torah is from great scholars. The Talmud teaches, "Even the mundane conversation of scholars provides useful material for study." [3]

When I was a student at the rabbinical school of the Jewish Theological Seminary, Rabbi Louis Finkelstein, chancellor, would often tell the story of his application for admission to JTS. He was asked by Dr. Solomon Schechter, "Why do you want to study here?"

Finkelstein answered, "to study great Jewish books."

"No," answered Schechter, "you come here to learn from great men."

This is the thrust of our Mishnah. It is from great teachers that one learns not only the teachings of tradition, but from the lives of

1 *Avot,* p. 32
2 *Avot* 1:2
3 Tractate Sukkah 21b

the great teachers who impart them.

When I read this Mishnah I think of my experience of the year I spent at Hebrew University, my junior year of Seminary study (1962-63). One of the guest speakers who inspired our group of rabbinical students was Professor Norman Bentwich. [(4)] Bentwich said many memorable things in his brief visit, but one thing sticks in my mind as if it were yesterday. He said that growing up in England his father had many important guests at his home. His home was "a meeting place for Sages."

Among the many people whom Bentwich remembers visiting his father's home were none less than Theodor Herzl and Ahad Ha'Am. Any wonder that Norman Bentwich grew up to be a leading professor at the Hebrew University, and held many other important positions in the Zionist movement.

"In the dust of their feet."

In ancient times, students sat on the floor, drinking in the wisdom of their teachers. Metaphorically, sitting in the dust can imply being humble during the experience of listening to great scholars.

"Sit in the dust of their feet."

The Hebrew word for "sit in the dust, – *mitabek*," is similar to the Hebrew root for the word in Genesis 32:25, when Jacob *wrestles* with the angel. Some interpret this midrashically, that to get the most of the Torah words one hears, it is important to struggle (wrestle) with their ideas and absorb them, not just listen to words without struggling to capture their full meaning.

Arthur Waskow's book is titled *God Wrestling*, for good reason. A student should make her/his learning deep, personal, a gut-wrenching struggle to take in the deeper meanings of the teachings.

"With thirst..."

A student who wants to derive the maximum from the words of teachers/scholars, must be enthusiastic, actively involved in the learning process. Water is often an apt metaphor in rabbinic parlance for Torah.

In one (of many such passages) the Talmud states: [(5)]

---

4 1883-1971

5 Tractate Bava Kama 82a

With regard to the verse, "And Moses led Israel onward from the Red Sea … and they went three days in the wilderness, and found no water." [(6)] Those who interpret verses metaphorically said that water here is referring to nothing other than Torah, as it is stated metaphorically, concerning those who desire wisdom: "Ho, everyone who thirsts, come for water." [(7)]

Humans cannot live without water, which constitutes 60% of the human body, and some 75% of the brain and heart. The Jew's need for Torah is not less than the need for life-sustaining water. A student should always be thirsty for more Torah, and never be satisfied, no matter how much knowledge one has gained.

Furthermore, Torah should be like fresh water, not stale drink. As Rashi teaches on Deuteronomy 11:13, our attitude to Torah should be as new to the learner as if she/he received it today. [(8)]

When two Jews accidentally meet and one will say in the spirit of the Talmud, and often in Yiddish, to the other: "*Nu, sogt mir a stickel Toire* – Quick! Tell me a new insight in the Torah or Talmud! Did we ever hear two people meet and one asking the other to tell him quickly "a stickel Shakespeare" because there is no greater joy? [(9)]

1:13 – A name made great is a name destroyed. One who does not increase one's knowledge loses it. One who does not study deserves to die, and one who makes worldly use of the crown of Torah passes away.

While there are many ways to achieve Torah knowledge, live by it, teach it, and keep it prominent in one's life, the advice in this Mishnah enumerates some of the ways that using, or not using, Torah in the wrong way can be dangerous.

Using one's acquisition of Torah knowledge, becoming a recognized expert and scholar in Torah matters, can easily lead to arrogance. "Pride goes before destruction, a haughty spirit before a

6 Exodus 15:22

7 Isaiah 55:1

8 Sifre Devarim 58

9 Rabbi Nathan Lopes Cardozo

fall." [10] To which Shakespeare in Macbeth adds this description of such pride, "Vaulting ambition which o'erleaps itself."

In learning and teaching Torah, a humble spirit and pure motives are significant components. Selfish motives and self-aggrandizement will not aid in the proliferation of Torah, and will only bring harm to its promoters. "A good name is rather to be chosen than great wealth, and grace is better than silver and gold", [11] and "A good name is better than precious oil." [12]

"One who does not increase one's knowledge loses it."

There is no stasis in the workings of the human mind. Neither is there in the observance of mitzvot or the practice of kindness. Rabbi Reuven Bulka writes, "In human striving there is no neutral gear. It is either forward or reverse." [13] It is common knowledge in educational theory that if one does not increase knowledge, what is learned is quickly forgotten. I can testify to this in my study of language. I studied French in high school and college, and continue to use it on occasion in travel and reading. While my French is far from perfect, I retain much of what I learned. On the other hand, I studied German for a short while, and have not continued to use the little I learned, and have thus forgotten all that I learned.

"One who does not increase one's knowledge loses it."

Albert Einstein taught a similar thought when he said, "Life is like riding a bicycle. To keep your balance you must keep moving."

"One who does not increase one's knowledge loses it."

Some commentators claim that the meaning here is that by not adding to the accumulated store of human culture, we diminish its ultimate value. Each generation must take it upon themselves to enrich the large accretion of knowledge and culture, lest it deteriorate and diminish.

"One who does not study deserves to die."

Without Torah life becomes meaningless, and one's life

10 Proverbs 16:18
11 Proverbs 22:1
12 Ecclesiastes 7:1
13 *As A Tree By the Waters*, p. 41

deteriorates spiritually. The Sages teach that study of Torah is the most effective means of eradicating evil in our lives. "If you are occupied with Torah, you will not be delivered into the power of the *yetzer ha-ra* [the evil impulse].... If the *yetzer ha-ra* meets you, drag it to the house of study. [14]

"Happy are the Jewish people, when they are engaged with Torah and kind deeds, the evil impulse is delivered into their power and they are not delivered into its power." [15]

"One who does not study deserves to die."

Some translate, "One who does not teach deserves to die." Rabbi Menahem Schneerson, the last Lubavitch Rebbe [16] taught that "Just as the material blessings of the rich person are not really his – he is merely God's treasurer through whom charity is distributed to the poor – likewise, one who possesses the blessings of Torah knowledge must realize that he is entrusted with such riches in order to convey it to others." [17]

1:15 – Make your Torah study a fixed practice.

Make Torah study a permanent fixture in your daily life. As we recite in the Maariv (evening) service on a daily basis, the words of Torah "are our life, and the length of our days, on them will we meditate day and night." Bartenura emphasizes this message by suggesting that we make study our first priority, and when tired, then do our work for sustenance, not the opposite. *Avot d'Rabbi Natan* suggests engaging in Torah study consistently, not just when one is in the mood.

Study of Torah is so important that we must make it a fixed part of our daily routine, not something random, casual or occasional. It should also not be seasonal: study during vacation periods, or when work is slow. Thus, in Avot 2:5, we read similar guidance, "Do not say, 'When I am free I will study,' for you may never have the time."

---

14 Tractate Kiddushin 30b

15 Tractate Avodah Zara 5b

16 Brooklyn, New York, d. 1994

17 Rabbi Yosef Marcus, *Pirkei Avot*, p. 38

An old book saved from the millions burned by the Nazis, and now housed at the YIVO library in New York, bears the stamp THE SOCIETY OF WOODCHOPPERS FOR THE STUDY OF MISHNA IN BERDICHEV. That the men who chopped wood in Berdichev, an arduous job that required no literacy, met regularly to study Jewish law demonstrates the ongoing pervasiveness of study of the Oral Law in the Jewish community.

I remember reading of a banker in Eastern Europe who kept a "shtender" (a lectern, or reading desk, with a slanted top, on which a Talmud volume is placed for study, or often for reading aloud) in the back room, so he could capture every free moment in Torah study. In Israel, I often see serious students holding a holy book on a bus or train, so as not to waste a second without increasing their Torah knowledge. On occasion, I see someone reading a holy book while walking on the street.

In 1923 Rabbi Meir Shapiro of the Lublin (Poland) Yeshivah initiated a program of daily study of the 2711 pages of the Babylonian Talmud in a cycle of seven and a half years.

Today hundreds of thousands of Jews around the world participate in this amazing program. What a wonderful unifying factor it is among Jews in today's complex society.

The Talmud teaches that when departing this world a person is brought to judgment and will be asked some important questions, of which the second is about setting aside fixed hours for Torah study: (18)

- Did you conduct business honestly?
- Did you set fixed times for Torah study?
- Did you engage in procreation?
- Did you hope for salvation?
- Did you engage in serious discussion of wisdom?

While the simple, seemingly obvious meaning of the Mishnah is, as discussed above, to make Torah study regular, there are several other possible interpretations. One is to make your Torah your own, not that of your parents. Each generation should establish a connection to Jewish life that it can feel passionately about, and not just routinely accept the way one's parents thought and acted.

18 Tractate Shabbat 31a

Another interpretation is that one's acceptance of Torah is fixed forever, never changing. As Maimonides wrote in the ninth of his thirteen principles of the Jewish faith, "I believe with perfect faith that this Torah will not be exchanged, and that there will never be any other Torah from the Blessed Creator." In other words, Torah is fixed and absolute, there is no time when it becomes inappropriate or irrelevant.

Another interpretation is for those who made halakhic (legal) decisions – namely, that one must have a fixed reading of Torah laws, not a lenient one for oneself, and a more strict one for others.[19]

Finally, one interpretation of the word "fixed" is that Torah values should be fixed in our mind, planted firmly, so they are translated into action, not just intellectual understanding. The Hebrew word for "fixed" is the same as the word in the blessing on affixing a mezuzah. Just as we "nail" a mezuzah in the doorpost, we should "nail," or affix Torah laws and ideas into our way of life.

1:16 – Get yourself a teacher, remove yourself from doubt.

Is this a repetition of 1:6, "Find for yourself a teacher"? Commentators say not. This Mishnah focuses more specifically on finding a teacher who can help you decide matters of Jewish Law (Maimonides). In making legal decisions it is important not to leave doubt in a questioner's mind.

"Remove yourself from doubt."

The statement reminds those who deal in matters of halakhah (Jewish law) that precision is important in such areas. Others take a broader view of the concept of doubt in this Mishnah. Rabbi Yosef Marcus explains the matter in these words:[20] "The *gematria* of Amalek is equal to that of *safek*, 'doubt.' Like Amalek, who attacked the Israelites in the desert despite all the open miracles God had displayed in Egypt, there is an Amalek within us that pours cold water on our spiritual enthusiasm with cynical, doubt-inducing thoughts. One of the ways of liberating ourselves from Amalek's doubt is by acquiring a teacher, i.e., a saintly Rebbe."

19 *Avot d'Rabbi Natan*
20 *Pirkei Avot*, p. 41

One must distinguish between areas of life and thought where doubt is a hindrance and doubt is an asset. Our Mishnah refers to specific areas of Halakhah, such as kashrut, in which certainty is called for. On the other hand, in areas of theology, doubt can be a positive step toward faith. Julia Baird, in the *New York Times* (September 14, 2014) writes:

> As Christopher Lane argued in "The Age of Doubt," the explosion of questioning among Christian thinkers in the Victorian era transformed the idea of doubt from a sin or lapse to necessary exploration. Many influential Christian writers, like Calvin and C.S. Lewis, have acknowledged times of uncertainty. The Southern writer Flannery O'Connor said there was "no suffering greater than what is caused by the doubts of those who want to believe," but for her, these torments were "the process by which faith is deepened."

Indeed, in the area of thought, doubt is often an important step towards a deepened faith. Elie Wiesel tells this story about faith and doubt: [21]

> A young Hasid came to see Rebbe Pinhas.
>
> "Help me, Master," he said. "I need your advice. I need your support. My distress is unbearable; make it disappear ... So strong are my doubts that I no longer know who I am, nor do I care to know. What am I to do, Rebbe? Tell me, what am I to do?"
>
> "Go and study," said Rebbe Pinhas of Koretz. "It's the only remedy I know ... Torah is the answer."
>
> "But I am unable even to study. So shaky are my foundations, so all-pervasive my uncertainties, that my mind finds no anchor, no safety. It wanders and wanders, and leaves me behind. I open the Talmud and contemplate it endlessly, aimlessly. For weeks and weeks I remain riveted to the same page, to the same problem. I cannot go farther, not even by a step, not even by a line. What must I do, Rebbe, what can I do to go on?"
>
> Rebbe Pinhas of Koretz tells his Hasid: "You must know, my friend, that what is happening to you also happened to

21 *Somewhere a Master*, pp. 11-12

me. When I was your age I stumbled over the same obstacles. I, too, was filled with questions and doubts ... I tried study, prayer, meditation. In vain. My doubts remained doubts. Worse: they became threats. Then one day I learned that Rebbe Israel Baal Shem Tov would be coming to our town. Curiosity led me to the *shtibl,* where he was receiving his followers. I entered just as he was finishing the *Amidah* prayer. He turned around and saw me, and I was convinced that he was seeing me, me and no one else. The intensity of his gaze overwhelmed me, and I felt less alone. And strangely, I was able to go home, open the Talmud, and plunge into my studies once more.

"You see," said Rebbe Pinhas of Koretz, "the questions remained questions. But I was able to go on."

The Rebbe reminded his young Hasid that doubt and uncertainty are part and parcel of the human experience. The remedy is not to give up, not to despair, but rather to learn, to persevere, to recognize that we will never uncover all the answers, and to realize, that we, too, like Rebbe Pinhas, can go on, not resolving all of the problems that surround us, but nonetheless we can make a vital contribution to those around us, by devoting heart and soul to the task that was first articulated in every single prayer service of the year – *LeTaken Olam B'Malkhut Shaddai* – to the task of bringing this world closer to the Kingdom of God.

Rabbi Nathan Lopes Cardozo [(22)] writes about the importance of doubt as a prerequisite to true faith:

"Once we realize that uncertainty was part of the biblical personality, we will have a much better grasp of the text and what Judaism is actually claiming. But this is only possible when we find ourselves challenged by those very existential doubts.

"There is nearly nothing greater than the free flow of doubt in today's society. It offers us unprecedented opportunities to rediscover *real* religiosity. In contrast, the quest for certitude paralyzes the search for meaning.

22 Jerusalem, b. 1946

> Uncertainty is the very condition that impels man to develop his spiritual and intellectual capacity. Sure, this is a risky undertaking, but there is no authentic life choice that is risk free. Life means constantly moving and growing, whereas organic matter that fails to shift and grow decays and will eventually die. So it is with man's religious life. The role of religion is to accommodate the blossoming of the human soul and to prevent man from descending into a place of spiritual stagnation….
>
> "To have faith is to live with unresolved doubts, prepared to rise above ourselves and our wisdom. Looking into the Jewish tradition with its many debates, one clearly understands that those who deny themselves the comfort of certainty are much more authentic than those who are sure.
>
> "Faith means that we worship and praise God before we affirm His existence; we respond before we question. Man can die for something even as he is unsure of its true existence, because his inner faith tells him it is right to do so. This honest admission of doubt is not only the very reason why it is possible to be religious in modern times; it is the actual stimulus to do so."

Rabbi Emanuel Rackman, [23] a prominent modern Orthodox rabbi, wrote this:

> "Judaism encourages doubt even as it enjoins faith and commitment. A Jew dare not live with absolute certainty, because certainty is the hallmark of the fanatic and Judaism abhors fanaticism, and because doubt is good for the human soul ... God had His own reasons for denying us certainty with regard to His existence and nature. One apparent reason is that man's certainty with regard to anything is poison to his soul. Who knows this better than moderns who have had to cope with dogmatic Fascists, Communists, and even scientists?" [24]

---

23 New York, d. 2008

24 In Milton Himmelfarb, ed., *The Condition of Jewish Belief*

2:2 – It is good to combine Torah study with a worldly occupation, for the effort involved in both makes one forget sin. Torah study without an occupation will in the end fail and lead to sin.

Many ancient rabbis shared their time with a worldly occupation and Torah study. Hillel was a wood-cutter, Shamai a builder, Rabbi Yehoshua a blacksmith, Rabbi Haninah a shoemaker, Rabbi Huna a water carrier, Rabbi Abba a tailor, Others were carpenters, tailors, well-diggers, surveyors, tent-makers, farmers, merchants, and whiskey distillers. In modern times many ordained rabbis choose to be involved in business ventures, and earn their rabbinic *semikhah* [rabbinic ordination] purely for the knowledge it brings.

The Talmud teaches that a father must teach his son a trade, and any father who does not, teaches him banditry. This may sound harsh, but the inference is that one who does not sustain oneself in a respectable occupation may resort to unhealthy avenues to support himself. [25]

The Sages insisted on the combination of study and an occupation for many reasons. As the old Frank Sinatra song goes, "they go together like a horse and carriage…You can't have one without the other." Study of Torah as an exclusive way of life tends to make Torah abstract and unrelated to the world – ineffective. The purpose of Torah study is to translate what one learns into practice, to utilize the moral lessons from Torah in carrying out its teachings in the real world. Torah divorced from worldly affairs makes Torah irrelevant.

On the other hand, busying oneself with one's business or profession denies the person the insights of Torah values in carrying out one's occupation or vocation. Combining the two fashions a creative symbiosis. Torah together with a worldly occupation is a deterrent against poor conduct. As our Mishnah teaches, "*the effort involved in both makes one forget sin.*" One who engages is serious study and hard work will have little time for improper conduct.

Some commentators translate Hebrew "*derekh eretz*," (literally, "the way of the earth"), in other ways than "a worldly occupation." The phrase can also mean good manners, proper etiquette, ethical behavior.

25 Tractate Kiddushin 29a

The Baal Shem Tov comments that any Torah study that does not eventuate into the "work" of loving other people is for naught.

Rabbi Shlomo P. Toperoff quotes Rabbi Uri Strelisker, [26] "We are taught by our Sages that the study of the Torah is good with 'the way of the earth.' We find that for all our necessities we must thank the earth. Without the earth we have neither food nor clothing. Yet we tread upon her, dig her, spit upon her, and the earth accepts every abuse without complaint. The student of the Torah should adopt these 'ways of the earth'. No matter how great his opinion is sought and esteemed, he should consider himself lowly and should accept debasement from anyone without complaint or anger."

Rabbi Ismar Schorsch describes a midrash in which there is a partnership between two of the sons of Jacob, Yissakhar and Zevulun. Writes Prof. Schorsch: " [Jacob] envisioned a division of labor. The tribe of Issachar would one day be sedentary, devoting itself wholly to the study of Torah. From its midst would spring the teachers, scholars and judges who would imbue society with the spirit of Torah. Hence, Jacob lavishes praise on Issachar. [27] In contrast, Zebulun is depicted as mercantile and mobile, a rank of a lower order in a culture of learning. And yet, Jacob speaks of them first because their wealth is earmarked to support the studies of Issachar. The merchants of Zebulun are the silent partners, the great enablers that ensure the transmission of Judaism. Without adequate funding, the study of Torah soon withers."

In other words, as often happened in Jewish history, a wealthy lover of learning provides the funds for the scholar to continue his studies and writing without the worry of earning a living. This is another way of combining Torah with "*derekh eretz*" ("a worldly occupation"). Some examples are Maimonides, perhaps the greatest Jewish scholar of medieval times, and his younger brother David, who ran an international jewel business, and who supported his older brother until his untimely death in a tragic shipwreck on his way to India. In more recent times, the wealthy Zalman Schocken became the patron of Israel's Nobel-prize winner, Shmuel Yosef Agnon, who spent most of his creative years with no worry of sustenance due to the benevolent financial support of Schocken.

26 Hasidic, d. Poland 1826

27 Genesis 30

There are more examples, in a different mode, of "Torah combined with a worldly occupation."

2:6 – A boor cannot be sin-fearing, nor can an ignoramus be pious. A shy person cannot learn, nor can an impatient one teach.

This Mishnah lists the common failings of teachers and students.

"A boor cannot be sin-fearing."

A *boor* in Hebrew is part of an expression, "*sdeh boor*," an uncultivated field. In other words, an uncultured person. Like such a field, a person who is a "boor" is one who has little chance of fruition, no possibility of spiritual growth. Various commentators define a "boor" as one who has neither wisdom nor character, one who is entirely empty like a barren field. Such a person has little chance of being sin-fearing, and probably is ignorant of the difference between a good deed and a sin.

"Nor can an ignoramus be a Hasid (pious)."

Piety is a very high ideal in Jewish tradition. In another Mishnah (5:10) we read: A Hasid is one who says "what's mine is yours, and what's yours is yours." That is, one who goes beyond the letter of the law. The Zohar, the mystical commentary on the Torah, teaches that a Hasid is one who acts lovingly toward his Creator.

"A shy person cannot learn."

Being shy, or humble, is a good trait, except in the process of learning. "Shyness (humility, meekness) leads to fear of sin" (Tractate Nedarim 20a). The implication is that one who is too shy to ask questions will not reach the level of deep understanding. Probing, investigating, exploring, analyzing, and searching are actions that lead to a more intense understanding of what a teacher expounds.

"Nor can an impatient one teach...."

One of the most important qualities of a teacher is patience. Often it requires repeating a teaching over and over. Maimonides translates the word "*kapdan*" ("impatient") as a "perfectionist." One who gets angry at every mistake does not possess the quality of an effective teacher. The Talmud states [28] that Rabbi Perida, an outstanding and patient teacher, repeated his lesson four hundred times until his student understood. For his patience, the Blessed Holy One rewarded him with a place in the World-to-Come.

2:8 – The more Torah, the more life. The more study, the more wisdom ... Whoever acquires for himself words of Torah acquires for himself life in the World to Come.

2:9 – If you have learned much Torah, take no special credit for yourself, for it was for this that you were created.

This Mishnah summarizes the Sages' view of life. The Torah, and all its commentaries (Talmud, Tosafot, medieval and modern elaborations, all built on the Torah) is the basis of Jewish values. With it, there is life, without it life, in the view of the Sages and all serious Jews, is deprived of genuine meaning.

Proverbs 2:1-5 sums it up well:

> My son, if you accept my words
> And treasure up my commandments –
>
> If you make your ear attentive to wisdom
> And your mind open to discernment –
>
> If you call to understanding
> And cry aloud to discernment –
>
> If you seek it as you do silver
> And search for it as for treasures –
>
> Then you will understand the fear of the Lord
> And attain knowledge of God.

"The more wisdom..."

In explanation of "wisdom," Maimonides wrote in a letter to

28 Tractate Eruvin 54b

his son, "Cleverness may serve its own profit, concentrate on its own fame, staying cold and heartless in the face of another's want. Wisdom of the heart brings happiness to our fellow-humans, drying tears from his face and lending strength to his efforts. The moon shines but it lacks warmth, its light may be brilliant and cold; this may be compared to cleverness without human sympathy. Wisdom, on the other hand, is like the resplendent sun – the sun of kindness with health on its wings."

"Life in the World to Come..."

The act of study offers a foretaste of life in the World to Come. Further, a teacher's influence goes beyond the grave. In the collection of stories of which I am co-editor, *Chicken Soup for the Jewish Soul*, this is one of my favorite stories:

An Audience Yet Unborn

Rabbi Mordechai Kamenetzky

There is a delightful story about a Rosh Yeshivah, the head of a rabbinical seminary. His name was Rabbi Shlomo Hyman, the first dean of Yeshiva Torah Vadaat, who had a most amazing way of teaching his students. Unlike the dry lectures given by many brilliant scholars, he would shout with almost breathless rapture as he explained the Talmud and its commentaries. His eyes would sparkle and his arms would wave as he expounded Talmudic theory. After the class he would almost collapse from the exertion.

On one particular snowy day back in the early 1940s, only four boys came to class. Nevertheless, Rabbi Hyman delivered his lecture as if the room was packed with hundreds of students. Beads of sweat rolled down his face as he passionately argued points of law to the incredulous four boys. As he paused to catch his breath, one of the boys mustered his courage and beseeched the Torah Giant.

"Rebbe, please – there are only four of us."

The rabbi's eyes widened. "You think I'm giving this class for four boys? I am giving this class to hundreds of boys. I'm giving this class to you, your students, their students, and their students!"

"Take no special credit for yourself, for it was for this that you were created."

"It was said of Rabban Yohanan, the author of this Mishnah, that he mastered all of Scripture, Mishnah, Gemara, halakhah, Midrash, scriptural exegesis, astronomical cycles, gematria, the speech of the angels, the secrets of plants, the parables about launderers and foxes, Ezekiel's vision of the Chariot, and all the discussions of the Talmud.[29] It is therefore appropriate for him to say, 'If you have learned much Torah, do not take credit for yourself.'"[30]

"It was for this that you were created."

"Learning is preeminent over all other activities in Jewish life. In this respect, Jews were unique in antiquity, for they had a passion for learning in which all were invited to participate. In the later period of Greek civilisation learning was the prerogative of certain individuals, and in Rome learning was not an essential ingredient in the curriculum of the State. In Judea alone, learning was included in the programme of the day and people vied with each other to master more and more learning".[31]

3:3 – When two people sit together and no words of Torah pass between them, they are regarded as a company of scoffers ... But when two people sit together and words of Torah do pass between them, the Divine Presence rests with them.

3:4 – Three who eat at one table, and do not speak words of Torah, are as if they had eaten of sacrifices of dead idols ... However, three who eat at one table and speak words of Torah, it is as if they had eaten at God's table.

"Words of Torah"

Rabbi Samson Raphael Hirsch writes, "We believe...that the meaning of *divrei Torah* [words of Torah] would include not only

29 Sukkah 28 and commentaries there

30 Rabbi Yosef Marcus, *Pirkei Avot,* p. 61

31 Rabbi Shlomo P. Toperoff, *Avot,* pp 102-103

the actual teaching contained in the Torah itself, but also everything else that derives from Torah for the fashioning of human affairs, as well as anything that is shaped in accordance with the Torah's teachings and is fulfilled in accordance with the spirit of the Law of God. But those who, instead of turning their thoughts to the serious things of life, in the broadest sense, waste their leisure time on frivolity and worthless trifles, their assembly is indeed classed by the Mishna as *moshav letzim* [a company of scoffers] even if, in fact, their words are not, strictly taken, in contempt of the Torah."[32]

"Between them"

It is not enough for each person at the table to study Torah, they must exchange words of Torah "between them." The Talmud teaches: [33] "One who could occupy oneself with the Torah but does not do so is counted among those of whom it is said, "that he despised the word of God."[34]

The morning prayers in the traditional *siddur* include the words "*la-asok b'divray Torah*," meaning to *occupy* oneself with words of Torah. It is not enough just to study the Torah, people must grapple, wrestle, and struggle to wrest the deeper meanings from every sentence, every word, of Torah.

"This Mishnah reflects the Sages' great insight that the destruction of the Temple signaled a change in the nature of God's presence from high-tension, sometimes even dangerous, but in a limited number of places (particularly the Temple), to a "lower-voltage," but in a wider number of places. When God is self-limited, allowing the Temple to be destroyed and become more "hidden," one could tap into His presence by studying or exchanging words of Torah. Even if only two people study Torah together, the Divine Presence would be discovered to be there."[35]

Rashi argues that reciting the *Birkat HaMazon* (Grace after Meals) fulfills this demand, since it contains several verses of Scripture. Others say that it is best not to rely on *Birkat HaMazon*, but add more words of Torah.

---

32 *Chapters of the Fathers*, p. 41

33 Tractate Sanhedrin 99a

34 Numbers 15:31

35 Rabbi Yitz Greenberg, *Sage Advice*, p. 113

The sharing of words of Torah at the table elevates the experience of dining to a level of holiness, truly making the table an altar. The Talmud reminds us of this teaching: "At the time that the Temple stood the altar atoned for a man, now his table atones for him." [36]

In modern times, sharing *divray Torah* (teachings) at dining or at meetings (such as synagogue board meetings) has become a common, and often expected practice. An acquaintance of mine, age 91, who lives in a nursing home, recently emailed me for assistance in writing a *d'var Torah* [Torah lesson]. There is a rotation in the home, each resident delivering a *d'var Torah* every Friday. Out of curiosity, I googled "How to Give a *d'var Torah*," and dozens of websites came up. This reflects the widespread practice of having lay, as well as rabbinic, teachers deliver words of Torah at almost any venue where Jews gather, including at meals.

4:6 – One who learns in order to teach will be given the opportunity to learn and to teach. One who learns in order to do will be given the opportunity to learn, teach, keep and do.

4:8 – One who honors the Torah will be honored by humanity. One who disgraces the Torah will be disrespected by humanity.

These two Mishnayot focus on the importance on living Torah values, not only studying them. In 4:8 we find that those who live Torah values will be respected by their Jewish and non-Jewish neighbors and friends.

4:11 – Whoever keeps the Torah when poor will eventually keep it in wealth. Whoever neglects the Torah when wealthy will eventually neglect it in poverty.

Rabbi Abraham J. Tweski comments: "Several commentaries challenge this interpretation of the Mishnah, because it is evident that many devoted Torah scholars and people who were meticulous in observance of Torah lived in poverty all their lives. Where then is the fulfillment of the Mishnah's promise? They therefore say that the Mishnah is not making a promise. Rather, it is making a statement, that if a person observed Torah when he was in poverty,

36 Tractate Hagigah 27a

he will likely continue to observe Torah if his fortune changes and he becomes wealthy. However, if someone was not observant of Torah when he was wealthy, he is unlikely to observe Torah if he falls into poverty." [37]

4:18 – Exile yourself to a place of Torah, and do not assume that it will come after you.

Rabbi Abraham Yitzhak Kook elaborates on the need for community to live a life of Torah:

> Part of the characteristic of Torah is that it recognizes the need for a social life with friendships, which bring to the world a good life within society. This is particularly rewarding when one's social group consists of good and scholarly people. Separation from other people and extreme asceticism, which is the approach of a significant portion of those people who, of their own, have sough closeness to HaShem, is a foreign idea to the Torah. For that reason, if one wants to acquire knowledge of Torah, he will succeed specifically by joining together with a group of learners, which shows the gains of avoiding isolation." [38]

Rabbi Yehudah HaNasi, [39] who was head of his own *yeshivah* (academy), advised his son to study for twelve years at another yeshivah. [40] In the days of the Talmud, scholars from *Eretz Yisrael* traveled to Babylon, the center of Torah learning, to study, and some from Babylon came to study with great scholars in *Eretz Yisrael* (the Land of Israel). [41]

It is very common in modern times for parents to send their children to live in place where there are better places to study Torah. Among my friends, I am aware of two friends of mine who sent their children to live with their grandparents in order that they could attend schools with intensive programs of Jewish learning.

37 *Visions of the Fathers*, pp. 222-223
38 *Ein Ayah, B'rakhot* 9:340-41
39 Editor of the Mishnah, d. 217 CE
40 Tractate Niddah 14b
41 Tosafot on Tractate Kiddushin 29a

The children would return to their parents' homes on weekends, when convenient. It is a frequent pattern among very traditional families to make great sacrifices in order to insure a school with serious learning opportunities.

4:25 – When you learn as a child, what is it like? Like ink written on fresh paper. When you learn in old age, what is it like? Like ink written on erased paper.

This Mishnah reflects more ancient wisdom, such as the biblical book of Proverbs (22:6): "Train a lad in the way he ought to go; and when he is old he will not depart from it." And before that the Torah admonishes us: "Impress them [these teachings] upon your children…." [(42)]

Education for the young began in early Talmudic times. Truly, that man is remembered for the good, and his name is Yehoshua ben Gamla. If not for him the Torah would have been forgotten from the Jewish people. Initially, whoever had a father would have his father teach him Torah, and whoever did not have a father would not learn Torah at all. The Gemara explains: What verse did they interpret homiletically that allowed them to conduct themselves in this manner? They interpreted the verse that states: "And you shall teach them [*otam*] to your sons", [(43)] to mean: And you yourselves [*atem*] shall teach, i.e., you fathers shall teach your sons.

When the Sages saw that not everyone was capable of teaching their children and Torah study was declining, they instituted an ordinance that teachers of children should be established in Jerusalem. The Gemara explains: What verse did they interpret homiletically that enabled them to do this? They interpreted the verse: "For Torah emerges from Zion". [(44)] But still, whoever had a father, his father ascended with him to Jerusalem and had him taught, but whoever did not have a father, he did not ascend and learn. Therefore, the Sages instituted an ordinance that teachers of children should be established in one city in each and every region. And they brought the students in at the age of sixteen and at the age

42 Deuteronomy 6:6
43 Deuteronomy 11:19
44 Isaiah 2:3

of seventeen.[45]

In a hyperbolic statement, typical of our ancient Sages, "The world exists only through the breath of school children."[46]

Rabbi Yitz Greenberg explains this Mishnah thus: "It is better and easier to learn Torah as a child, when the mind is not as clogged and the openness to improvement and new thoughts is at its peak. One can learn Torah in old age, but 'the paper has been erased.' The mind is not as pristine, as sharp, or as retentive as it was in childhood."[47]

Dr. William Berkson explains,[48] "...the idea is not just that the young have better memories than the old, but also that there is a qualitative difference between the learning of the young and the old. What we learn as a child not only sticks, but is laid down as a framework, a set of lenses that we look through to interpret everything else. We understand that framework more deeply than anything else, and it forms a foundation for our other learning."

Another way to say the same thing is the old proverb, "Teaching Torah to the young is like engraving in stone, while teaching the old is like engraving in sand."

Rabbi Berel Wein relates this: "My wife taught fourth grade for twenty-five years. I, on the other hand, have always taught on a high school or post-high school, even graduate school level. I envy her achievements and lasting influence on her students, which I believe have been far greater than mine.[49]

5:26 – Turn it [the Torah] over and over, for everything is in it. Reflect on it, grow old and gray in it and do not stir from it, for there is no better portion for you than this.

This Mishnah reflects, again, the predominant place that Torah holds in the Jewish psyche. Not only is the Torah the central statement of Jewish ethics, history and tradition, this statement adds another dimension to Torah: it (Torah in its broadest sense,

45 Tractate Bava Batra 21a
46 Tractate Shabbat 119b
47 *Sage Advice,* p. 225
48 *Pirkei Avot,* p. 157
49 *Pirkei Avos,* p. 176

all Jewish knowledge) contains everything one needs to live a complete and meaningful life. The Torah and its commentaries up until this moment, contains an inexhaustible treasure of wisdom for anyone who wants to live a full Jewish life.

Other statements in the Talmud and elsewhere contain like-minded assertions. For example, "The Torah has seventy faces,"[(50)] meaning that the Torah has a limitless number of ways to understand its many layers of meaning. As we read in Joshua: "This book of the Torah shall not depart from your mouth, but meditate on it day and night."[(51)]

And in Avot we find: "the more Torah, the more life, the more study the more wisdom ... whoever acquires words of Torah acquires life in the World to Come .[(52)]

Rabbi Shlomo P. Toperoff claims that we can learn many things from "the Torah," including science, biology, zoology, genetics, agriculture, nutrition, medicine, astronomy, town planning, and more. One can learn both the revealed parts (*galui*) and the esoteric portions (*nistar*).

The Hebrew phrase "turn it" (*hafokh ba*) is repeated to emphasize its importance, to review it over and over. "One who reviews his studies one hundred times is not comparable to one who reviews his studies one hundred and one times."[(53)]

"For everything is in it."

Rabbi Joseph Hertz comments that "It is a complete guide to life," and proceeds to quote from the commentary of "*Lev Avot*:" In it without doubt, are history and tale; proverb and enigma; correction and wisdom; knowledge and discretion; poetry and word-play; conviction and counsel; dirge, entreaty, prayer, praise, and every kind of supplication; and all this in a Divine way is superior to all the prolix benedictions in human books; to say nothing of containing in its depths the Names of the Holy One... and secrets of being without end."

"Grow old and gray in it."

---

50 Midrash Bemidbar Rabbah 13:15

51 Joshua 1:8

52 Avot 2:8

53 Tractate Hagigah 9b

It has wisdom for people of all ages. In one's older years it has the power of rejuvenation.

Our Mishnah is best summarized in this anonymous Yiddish poem, one of my favorites, one that I quote often when I lecture in synagogues or other Jewish venues:

All I Got Was Words

When I was young and fancy free,
My folks had no fine clothes for me
All I got was words:

Gott tzu danken
Gott vet geben
Zoln mir leben un zein gezunt

When I was wont to travel far,
They didn't provide for me a car
All I got was words:

Geh gezunt Geh pamelech
Hub a glickliche rayze

I wanted to increase my knowledge
But they couldn't send me to college
All I got was words:

Hub saychel
Zei nischt kein narr
Torah iz di beste schorah

The years have flown – the world has turned,
Things I've gotten, things I've learned,
Yet I remember:

Zog dem emes
Gib tzedokah
Hub rachmonas
Zei a mensch!

All I got was words.

Materialism

2:8 – The more flesh, the more worms. The more possessions, the more worries.

This Mishnah counsels moderation, which would prevent the excesses listed in this Mishnah. Maimonides wrote: "Let one practice over and over the actions promoted by the '*midah beinonit*' [the middle way, the golden mean], the mean between the extremes, and repeat them continually till they become easy and are no longer irritating to him, and so the corresponding temperaments will become a fixed part of his character" Further, "A Torah Sage should not be a glutton. Rather, he should eat food which will keep his body healthy, without overeating."[(1)]

Our Mishnah advocates avoidance of gluttony and overindulgence in sensual pleasures. "Do not toil to gain wealth; have the sense to desist."[(2)]

In the Torah we read of a stubborn and rebellious son, who is "a glutton and drunkard." [(3)] Obesity has been termed a modern epidemic, and is associated with an increase in diabetes, cardiovascular disease, sleep disorders, and has negative effects on a variety of other conditions, including psychological disorders. The fact that there are countless numbers of diets and companies that promote weight, such as Weight Watchers, is an indication of how widespread the problem has become. In Ecclesiastes, 5:11, we read, "A worker's sleep is sweet, whether he has much or little to eat, but the rich person's abundance does not let him sleep."

"The more flesh, the more worms."

The heavier the person, the more there is for the worms to consume. Rabbi Reuven P. Bulka comments, "One who overeats is likely to think twice if made aware that all the eating is only to feed the worms." Others suggest that "worms" refers to potential diseases that eventuate from obesity. The heavier the person, the

1 Mishneh Torah, Hilkhot Deot, chapter four
2 Proverbs 23:4
3 Deuteronomy 21:18-20

more susceptible she/he is to illness.

Rabbi Abraham J. Twerski, who is a physician and well-known rabbi, writes: "The human being is a composite of a physical body and a spiritual soul. The body is essentially an animal body, and if we observe nature closely we will find that animals generally do not indulge in excesses. For example, a lion or a tiger will kill its prey for food, but once the body's nutritional needs have been met, they stop eating. Animals in the wild do not become obese. When their natural needs are met, they abstain. It would be well if the human being attended to his physical needs as animals do, only to the degree that one's physiology and good health requires. An excess of food or drink, beyond the body's physiological needs, is likely to be harmful."

"The more possessions, the more worries."

Humans have an insatiable hunger for more. "If one has one hundred, he wants two hundred." [4] Modern society has created a materialistic ethic that drives people to "shop until they drop." Anyone who owns modern appliances or vehicles knows that the more "things" one owns, the more care, the more repair, the more updating and upgrading is required. To the point that our possessions own their owners, instead of the reverse.

In addition to the time consuming in caring for possessions there are several causes of "worries," such as the fear of loss, of theft, of being robbed or killed for one's possessions, or the fear of their value depreciating. This phrase, "the more possessions, the more worries," rings true in today's society more than it did when this was first written.

On the other hand, Judaism never counseled asceticism. A balanced view of physical possessions and a comfortable lifestyle can also lead to a more relaxed attitude. As Maimonides put it, all in moderation. Reaching the "*midah beinonit*," the golden mean, is the ideal.

Rabbi David Wolpe [5] writes on materialism: When the brothers meet, Esau tells Jacob, "I have much." Jacob responds by saying "I have enough" (lit. I have everything.)

4 Ecclesiastes Rabbah 1:34

5 Los Angeles, b. 1958

The scholar and ethicist Meir Tamari calls this "the economics of enough." We always want more; as Ecclesiastes teaches, "the eye never has enough of seeing nor the ear of hearing" – we might add, nor the hand of grasping. Yet beyond a certain point money and possessions are not what you need or even what you can use, but about salving the ego with more and more and more.

Many people in our communities have far more money than they or their families could possibly spend, and are nonetheless reluctant to contribute to charity. Others have celebrations so lavish that the spiritual meaning is drowned in awful opulence. This is not the economics of enough or even the economics of excess, it is the economics of egregiousness.

Money in this world should be not a cistern but a fountain. It can make the world better if used, not merely to fortify the walls of a shaky self-esteem by being amassed. Limitation and generosity are hallmarks of our tradition; rapacity and hoarding are the antithesis of Israel, who taught us the economics of enough.

This Mishnah concludes by offering antidotes to the excesses in consumption of food and drink, obsession with possessions, and other extravagances: a life filled with Torah, study, wisdom, counsel and charity.

2:17 – Let the money [or property] of your friend be as precious to you as your own.

One who is not materialistic or plagued by envy of another's money or possessions should treat her/his neighbor's property as he would treat his own. Maimonides teaches that treating another's property respectfully, in the same way one would treat their own, is the fulfillment of the biblical command, "You shall love your neighbor as yourself." (6)

The ArtScroll *Pirkei Avos Treasury* brings an interesting twist on this Mishnah. "A more emotional interpretation asks that we consider money given to charity as though it were spent on a personal need or desire. Such money actually remains our own, safely invested in our Heavenly bank account since we have not really parted with it. (7)

6 Leviticus 19:18

7 R' Yehoshua Heschel of Monostrich

Mitzvot

2:1 – Be as meticulous in the observance of a minor mitzvah as a major one, for you do not know the reward for each mitzvah.

Rabbi Abba bar Kahana said: "God says, 'Do not sit and weigh the mitzvot of the Torah...Do not say, "Since a particular mitzvah is significant, I will do it because its reward is great, and since another mitzvah is less significant, I won't do it." ' God did not reveal to His creations the reward for any particular mitzvah, so that they should perform *each* mitzvah with perfection... God did not reveal the reward for any mitzvah except for two: the hardest and the easiest. Honoring parents is the hardest, and its reward is long life, as the verse say: 'Honor your father and your mother so that your days may be lengthened...'." [(1)]

The easiest is sending away the mother bird. What is its reward? It is long life, as the verse says: Certainly send away the mother and take the chicks for yourself, in order that it will be good for you and you will have lengthened days. [(2)]

This Midrash seems to contradict other statements in Avot and other places in the Talmud. In Avot 1:3 we read: "Do not be like servants who serve their master on condition of receiving a reward. It is thus not unusual for the Sages to have different opinions on different subjects. In fact, this is the hallmark of the Talmud – the ability to disagree and yet have all opinions included. "Both these and these are the living words of God." [(3)]

One reason for not distinguishing between major and minor mitzvot is that doing one "minor" mitzvah may encourage someone to then do another and another and another, until the person performs many mitzvot she/he may not have done before. We can never completely predict the results of an action.

Some commentators claim that one can never know completely which mitzvot are "major" and which are "minor."

Another explanation is that the Mishnah is not only referring to

1 Exodus 20:12

2 Deuteronomy 22:7; Midrash Deuteronomy Rabbah 6:2

3 Tractate Eruvin 13b

"major" and "minor" mitzvot, but to the level of enthusiasm and devotion one has in performing different mitzvot.

4:2 – Run to do even a minor mitzvah, and flee from sin, for one mitzvah leads to another, and one sin leads to another – for the reward of a mitzvah is another mitzvah, and the reward of a sin is another sin.

"For the reward of a mitzvah is another mitzvah."

Similar ideas have been articulated in other cultures. Cicero, the Roman orator and philosopher [(4)] said, "Virtue is its own reward."

Commentators explain this Mishnah in several ways. The most common explanation is that one does not need a reward for a good deed. The good deed *(mitzvah)* is a reward in itself. Another explanation is that each good deed is followed by another one. Positive actions set in motion a pattern of good deeds that continue and multiply, in a kind of spiritual chain reaction.

"One sin leads to another... the reward of a sin is another sin."

The Scottish poet Robert Burns wrote:

Oh what a tangled web we weave
When first we practice to deceive.

In other words, every lie compels one to cover it with another lie. The punishment for a sin is having to sin again. Committing a transgression encourages one to commit other transgressions to hide the first one. Each bad deed dulls the conscience.

There are many Talmudic passages which convey a similar sense – that when one sins the first time, it easily become habitual. "Sins repeated are soon seen as permissible." [(5)] "The evil inclination is at first like a strand of a spider's web; and ultimately it is like the thick ropes of a wagon." [(6)]

"Initially, the evil inclination is called a traveler, then a guest, and ultimately, the homeowner." [(7)] And finally, "One who comes in order to sin, Heaven provides him with an opening to do so.

4 d. 43 CE
5 Tractate Yoma 86b
6 Tractate Sukkot 52a
7 Tractate Sukkot 52b

However, if he comes in order to become purified, not only is he allowed to do so, but they, in Heaven, assist him."[(8)]

Another explanation is that a sin committed influences the next generation to follow the ways of one's ancestors. Patterns of behavior in a family become repetitive.

Rabbi Toperoff comments: "the mitzvah is infectious for good. Similarly, the *averah* (transgression) is infectious for evil and drags the evil-doer into the mire."[(9)]

4:13 – One who performs a single mitzvah acquires for himself an advocate. One who commits a single transgression acquires for himself an accuser. Repentance and good deeds are a shield against punishment.

"An advocate."

Rashi explains that one who performs one mitzvah acquires one advocate, or character witness, before the Heavenly Court. Others say: before the court of public opinion. One who does mitzvot becomes known in the community as a decent human being.[(10)]

Bartenura comments that every mitzvah performed creates for a person an advocating angel, an angel of mercy. Of course, we all need angels for mercy when we are judged.

"Repentance and good deeds are a shield against punishment."

These fundamental acts, *mitzvot, teshuvah* and *maasim tovim*, [commandments, repentance and good deeds] are the very best advocates for us. When I was a student at the Jewish Theological Seminary, our professor, Rabbi Louis Finkelstein, would often say that these two acts, *teshuvah*[(11)] and *maasim tovim*, are the core of Judaism. He repeated this important statement often in class.

---

8 Tractate Shabbat 104a

9 p. 141

10 See also Tractate Shabbat 32a

11 See my book, *Forty Days of Repentance*, which presents a wealth of teachings on the doctrine of Teshuvah, for study between the first of the Hebrew month of Elul to the tenth of the month of Tishre – Yom Kippur

"Teshuvah."

This is one of Judaism's key doctrines. It is never too late to return. "In a *place* where a *baal teshuva* (spiritual returnee) *stands, even* a full *tzaddik cannot stand.*" (12)

"Teshuvah was created before the universe, because without it the world could not endure." (13)

"Great is Teshuvah for it brings healing to the world." (14)

Teshuvah is great since it brings healing to the world. (15)

Great is Teshuvah since it brings redemption to the world. (16)

Rabbi Joseph Hertz comments: "The Rabbis dwell especially on the text, 'And God saw their works, that they turned from their evil way; and God relented of the evil, which He said He would do unto them; and He did it not' (17) – not their fasting and sackcloth, but their 'works', i.e. good deeds, secured their pardon."

12 Tractate Brakhot 34b
13 Tractate Pesahim 54a
14 Tractate Yoma 86b
15 Tractate Rosh Hashanah 17b
16 Tractate Yoma 17b
17 Jonah 3:10

Particularism vs. Universalism

1:14 – If I am not for myself, who will be for me? And if I am only for myself, what am I? And if not now, when?

This Mishnah is one of the most oft-quoted aphorisms in the Talmud. It presents a unique balance between "particularism" and "universalism." There is a natural instinct to preserve ourselves, and an altruistic instinct to help others. The Mishnah advises wisely that taking care of one's own needs is a necessary prerequisite to caring for others. As George Bernard Shaw wrote, "A man's interest in the world is only the overflow of his interest in himself."

Rabbi Menahem Mendel [(1)] of Kotzk taught something that fleshes out this Mishnah in an interesting way: "If I am who I am because I am who I am, and you are who you are, then I am who I am and you are who you are. But if I am who I am because you are who you are, and you are who you are because I am who I am, then I am not I nor are you, you." [(2)] The Kotzker captures the idea in a novel way. In short, one has to establish one's own identity without dependence on another.

In the Talmudic value system, one must care for one's own needs first, not as a selfish act, but as a preparation for helping others. In distributing charity," if it is between one of the poor of your city and one of the poor of another city, the one of the poor of your city takes precedence." [(3)] In other words, your family comes first, and then others.

Hillel, author of this Mishnah, [(4)] acts on his own advice. The Midrash recounts this fascinating tale about Hillel taking care of his health: "The merciful man does good to his own soul," [(5)] this [refers to] Hillel the Elder, who, at the time that he was departing from his students, would walk with them. They said to him,

1 Poland, d. 1859

2 *Hasidic Wisdom*, ed. Simcha Raz, translated by Dov Peretz Elkins, p. 73

3 Tractate Bava Metzia 71a

4 Leviticus Rabbah 34:3

5 Proverbs 11:17

"Rabbi, where are you walking to?" He said to them, "To fulfill a commandment!" They said to him, "And what commandment is this?" He said to them, "To bathe in the bathhouse." They said to him: "But is this really a commandment?" He said to them: "Yes. Just like regarding the statues (lit. icons) of kings, that are set up in the theaters and the circuses, the one who is appointed over them bathes them and scrubs them.... I, who was created in the [Divine] Image and Form, as it is written, "For in the Image of God He made man," [6] even more so!

The American Quaker poet, John Greenleaf Whittier [7] wrote:

Heaven's gate is shut
To him who comes alone,
Save Thou a soul,
And it shall save thine own.

A perfect synthesis of caring for self and caring for others.

I remember from my frequent experiences on an airplane, the flight attendant, in preparation for take-off, would always say that in case of emergency, the oxygen mask will automatically appear in front of you.... "*If you are travelling with a child or someone who requires assistance, secure your mask on first, and then assist the other person.*" In other words, you cannot be helpful to anyone else unless you are in good shape yourself.

"And if I am only for myself, what am I?"

The well-known phrases in Jewish tradition, such as "*tikkun olam*," [repairing the world] and "*L'or goyim*," [a light to the nations] – reflect Judaism's concern for others. Repairing the world, being a light to the nations, are among the many Jewish value concepts that reflect the Jewish concern to serve others, i.e., universalism. We have a higher pedigree; we are the prime representatives of God, who is ultimate Truth. We embody the noblest traits, the highest standards of morality and goodness. It is we who were chosen to reveal the light of God, to set the standard

6 Genesis 9:6
7 d. 1892

for holy behavior.

"And if not now, when?"

The Mishnah ends with a warning to avoid procrastination. The demands of the hour call upon us to avoid putting off until tomorrow what needs to be done now. "If you neglect study one day, it will neglect you two days." [(8)]

The rabbis considered doing a mitzvah in a timely way is very important. "A mitzvah that presents itself to you, do not allow it to become sour." [(9)]

Rabbi Abraham ibn Ezra [(10)] wisely wrote: "The past is gone, the future has not yet arrived, and the present is as fleeting as the blink of an eye."

8 Jerusalem Talmud, Tractate Berakhot 9:8

9 Midrash Mekhilta, d'Rabbi Yishmael on Exodus 12:17

10 Spain, d. 1167

Peace

1:12 – Be among the disciples of Aaron, loving peace and pursuing peace. (1)

1:18 – On three things the world exists – on truth, justice, and peace, as it is said: Administer truth and the judgment of peace in your gates (2)

In 1:2 we find a different three ingredients: Torah, Divine worship, and acts of loving-kindness. Here we find: justice, truth, and peace. Rabbi Yonah of Gerona, (3) offers a reconciliation: the world was created for the sake of Torah, Divine worship and acts of loving-kindness. But the world is sustained by justice, truth and peace. It is noteworthy that the three ingredients in 1:2 focus mainly on Jewish themes, while our Mishnah is more universal.

"Our Mishnah issues three warnings here, each addressed to a different party in the judicial process. Justice is demanded of the judges, who must adjudicate fairly and without bias; truth must be the guiding light of the witnesses, upon whom the veracity of the entire process depends; peace is the banner beneath which the litigants must rally. Once the verdict is issued, all animosity between them must melt under the healing warmth of peace. By joyfully accepting the decision of the court, they will restore harmony to their lives." (4)

Truth can be compromised to preserve a higher value: peace. The Talmud gives this example: (5) "It was taught in the school of Rabbi Yishmael: Great is peace, as even the Blessed Holy One departed from the truth for it." As, initially it is written that Sarah said of Abraham: "And my lord is old," (6) and in the end it is written that

1 See our theme on "Kiruv"

2 Zechariah 8:16

3 Spain, d. 1263

4 *Beis Yosef* and *Midrash Shmuel. The Pirkei Avos Treasury,* ArtScroll, p. 55

5 Tractate Yevamot 65b

6 Genesis 18:12

God told Abraham that Sarah said: "And I am old."[7] God adjusted Sarah's words in order to spare Abraham hurt feelings that might lead Abraham and Sarah to quarrel." Affirming this approach is the statement, "All untruths are forbidden, but it is permitted to fudge for the sake of bringing peace between a person and his friend."[8]

Rabbi Shmuley Yanklowitz brings these wise words from Rabbi Ben-Zion Uziel, Sephardic Chief Rabbi of Mandatory Palestine and Israel, serving from 1939-1953: Uziel "taught that legal rulings must not only be intellectually correct, but also morally good." The Talmud teaches, 'Where there is strict justice, there is no peace; and where there is no peace, there is no strict justice!'"[9]

Peace is the climax of the famous three-part priestly blessing:[10]

May the Lord bless you and keep you.
May the Lord's face shine upon you and be gracious to you.
May the Lord lift up His face unto you and grant you peace.

Rabbi Abraham J. Twerski writes: "*Shalom* (peace) is without question the most important ingredient for a society's existence. Indeed, the Talmud states that God did not find any suitable receptacle for His blessings other than *shalom.*[11] This notwithstanding, even *shalom* must be qualified. A *shalom* that is without truth and law is not constructive....

"The *shalom* that is conducive to the healthy function of society and of the family unit is a *shalom* that is based on truth and law. There are no secrets, no cover-ups, no misinformation. There is a profound respect for the dignity and status of everyone – man, woman, and child. Only this kind of *shalom* is a receptacle for the Divine blessings."[12]

Other important and frequent references to "shalom" in the Jewish tradition should be mentioned:

---

7 Genesis 18:13

8 *Derekh Eretz Zuta, Perek HaShalom,* 5

9 Tractate Sanhedrin 6b; *Pirkei Avot: A Social Justice Commentary,* pp. 56-57

10 Numbers 6:23-27

11 Tractate Uktzin 3:12

12 *Visions of the Fathers,* p. 67

"I shall grant peace in the land, and you shall lie down untroubled by anyone." [13]

"Peace, peace, to the far and the near, said the Lord." [14]

"Seek peace and pursue it." [15]

"Peace upon Israel." [16]

Maimonides taught: "Great is peace, as the whole Torah was given in order to promote peace in the world, [17] as it is written 'Her ways are ways of pleasantness, and all her paths are peace.'" [18]

---

13 Leviticus 26:6
14 Isaiah 57:19
15 Psalms 34:15
16 Psalms 125:5
17 Laws of Hanukkah 4:14
18 Proverbs 3:17

Personal Qualities

4:1 – Who is wise? One who learns from everyone, as it is said, From all my teachers I gained wisdom. [1]

Who is strong? One who masters his evil impulse, as it is said, One who is slow to anger is better than the mighty, and he who rules over his spirit is better than he who conquers a city. [2]

Who is rich? One who rejoices in what he has, as it is said, When you eat from the labor of your hands, you will be happy and all will be well with you. [3]

Who is honored? One who honors others, as it is said, Those who honor Me, I will honor, but those who scorn Me will be dishonored. [4]

This Mishnah presents counter-cultural values for several of the most important values in human life. The Mishnah presents Torah values in place of secular value, in a counter-intuitive way. The themes are based on Jeremiah 9:22, Thus said the Lord:

Let not the wise man glory in his wisdom;
Let not the strong man glory in his strength;
Let not the rich man glory in his riches.
But only in this should one glory: In one's earnest devotion to Me. For I, the Lord, act with kindness, justice and equity in the world; For in these I delight – declares the Lord.

In other words, in terms of wisdom, power, wealth and honor, the Mishnah presents the Jewish definition of these values.

Let us examine each of the values one by one. First, *wisdom*. A person should be humble enough to be willing to learn from any source, even if the person's ideas are different, even if one does not like the person.

It was written of Hillel "that he had not neglected any of the words of the Wise. He studied all languages, even that of the mountains, hills, and valleys, of the trees and herbs, of beasts, wild

1 Psalms 119:99
2 Proverbs 16:32
3 Psalms 128:2
4 I Samuel 2:30

and tame; tales of demons, popular stories, and parables, he learned everything."[5]

When the Talmud discusses the different views of the Schools of Hillel and Shamai, it states that the views of the School of Hillel prevailed, because their disciples were kindly and humble, and mentioned the views of the School of Shamai before their own.[6]

When I lived in Princeton, New Jersey, the community was building a new community hospital. The CEO polled every worker before finalizing the plans for the new hospital – including the janitors, secretaries, and anyone who had anything to do with the hospital. No one was too low on the social or economic scale to offer suggestions to build the finest hospital in every aspect. As a result, the new hospital turned out to be one of the finest on the East Coast of the United States.

"Who is wise? One who learns from everyone."

The Mishnah does not say one who has learned, but who learns (present tense), from everyone. The process of learning is more important than the amount of knowledge gained. The classroom for such a one is the world.

The Maggid of Mezritch[7], a leading Hasidic teacher, said that we can learn even from a thief. He will keep trying again and again, and will not give up until he succeeds. And that we can learn from an infant, not to be idle, always smile, and when you want something, cry for it (our prayers should be accompanied by tears).

Next, let's look at *power*.

"Who is strong? One who masters his evil impulse."

The Mishnah does not ask to *destroy* the *yetzer ha-ra*, but to *master* it. It never goes away. Fighting the *yetzer ha-ra* is a lifelong battle. In some ways, the *yetzer ha-ra* has positive qualities. "Were it not for the evil inclination, a person would not build houses, would not marry, and would not bear children.[8]

True strength is when one turns an enemy into a friend.[9]

5 Tractate Sofrim 16:9

6 Tractate Eruvin 13b

7 Poland, d. 1772

8 Midrash Bereshit Rabbah 9:7

9 *Avot d'Rabbi Natan* 23:1

Next, *wealth*. The Mishnah does not describe the wealthy person as one who is "*satisfied*" with her/his lot, but one who is "*happy*" with his lot. "One who has one hundred desires two hundred". [10] The Mishnah describes one who is the opposite of greedy.

British scholar Bertrand Russell taught, "There is nothing as destructive of happiness as the habit of comparing oneself to others." Too often we imagine that the grass is greener on the other side of the fence, instead of enjoying our own gifts.

This Hasidic story about Reb Zusha [11] of Anipoli illustrates the lesson of the Mishnah:

> The brothers Rabbi Shmuel-Shmelke and Rabbi Pinhas remembered the words of the Mishnah, [12] One must bless on hearing evil tidings just as one blesses on hearing good tidings, and after that the words of the Talmud: The Mishnah's statement was only necessary to instruct us to accept bad tidings with the same joy with which we accept good tidings. [13]

They were reflecting and wavering on the matter:

Hasidism commands joy. The ancient Sages require accepting the evil tidings, not only in love but with joy ... how is it possible for a human being, for one of flesh and blood, to bless on evil tidings, and with joy, just as one blesses on good tidings? So they left Vilna, and traveled to Mezritch. They came to the room of the Maggid, Rabbi Dov Ber of Mezritch, immediately after the greeting, presented to him this question.

The Maggid said to them:

> A simple question like this even my Zusha can answer. Go ask him. The brothers looked at each other in surprise at this reply. They entered the *Bet Midrash* of the Maggid, and asked: Who is this Zusha? One of the group answered and pointed to a poor wretched man, standing near the oven, dancing and frolicking and reading the book of Psalms with lyrical emotion, and his face glowing with joy. And that was Rabbi Zusha of Anipoli.

They approached him and told him that the Maggid sent them to

10 Midrash Ecclesiastes Rabbah 1:34

11 Poland, d. 1800

12 Tractate Berakhot 54a

13 Tractate Berakhot 60b

him and presented to him their question.

> I am surprised, answered Rabbi Zusha in innocence, that our holy rabbi sent you to me. This question should be asked to one who once underwent punishment, to one who experienced some bad times in his life. A person like that can know if it is possible to accept bad things in joy and to make a blessing on it. Zusha never experienced bad things in his life, Heaven forbid. Zusha has only had goodness and kindness his whole life, and he always blesses for goodness. [(14)]

"The philosophy of wealth is read into the Hebrew word for a rich man, *ashir*, which consists of the [Hebrew] letters *ayin, shin, yod, resh*. These letters initial the words *ainayim*, eyes; *shinayim*, teeth, *yadayim*, hands and *raglayim*, feet. One who is blessed with the use of these limbs is indeed a rich person." [(15)]

"If you can't get what you want, then want what you can get." [(16)]

Who is Rich? Those who are content with their portion.

"No matter what their income, a depressing number of Americans believe that if they only had twice as much, they would inherit the estate of happiness promised them in the Declaration of Independence. The man who receives $15,000 a year is sure that he could relieve his sorrow if he only had $30,000 a year: the man with $1 million a year knows that all would be well if he had $2 million a year ... Nobody has enough." [(17)]

Finally, *honor*. It seems obvious that one who honors others will then be honoring oneself. Honoring others, and hence being honored by others, is the sum of the other three qualities – openness to learning from everyone, controlling one's impulses, and rejoicing in one's portion.

The Talmudic Sage, Nehuniah ben HaKaneh was once asked by his disciples:

---

14 Adapted from *The Holy Brothers: Rabbi Elimelekh and Rabbi Zusha of Anipoli*, ed. Simcha Raz, translated by Dov Peretz Elkins

15 *Avot*, Rabbi Shlomo P. Toperoff, p. 198

16 Rabbi Jacob Anatoli, Naples, d. 1256

17 Lewis Lapham, *Money and Class in America: Notes and Observations on Our Civil Religion*, 1988

In the merit of which virtue were you blessed with longevity? He said to them:

"In all my days, I never attained honor at the expense of my fellow's degradation. Nor did my fellow's curse ever go up with me upon my bed. If ever I offended someone, I made sure to appease him that day. Therefore, when I went to bed I knew that no one had any grievances against me. And I was always openhanded with my money."[18]

4:4 – Be very, very humble of spirit, for the end of a mortal is the worm [the grave].

The author of this Mishnah is probably quoting an older book, Ben Sirah (7:17) (also called Ecclesiasticus), part of the Apocrypha. Often important aphorisms are copied and repeated in different books and different cultures. My view is that if it is important enough to be copied, it is important enough to study again and again. In the case of this Mishnah, it is the only precept quoted in the name of its author, Rabbi Levitas, in the entire six orders of the Mishnah. Rabbi Elad-Appelbaum comments: "How fitting that Rabbi Levitas leaves us only this sentence, and we know of no other statements of his. In that taciturnity lies true humility! One sole sentence, carrying out in a mere eight [Hebrew] words a message of eternity."[19]

The subject of humility is prominent in biblical books. "Now Moses was a very humble man, more so than any other man on earth."[20] On this verse, *Humash Etz Hayyim* comments, "[Hebrew *anav*] applies to the weak and the exploited. It never means 'meek.'" True humility is not weakness, but strength of character.

In the book of the prophet Micah we find this famous verse: "He [God] has told you, O man, what is good, and what the Lord requires of you: Only to do justice and to love mercy, and to walk humbly with your God."[21]

The Sages also weigh in passionately on the subject of humility.

18 Tractate Megillah 28a

19 *Pirkei Avot Lev Shalem*, page 179

20 Numbers 12:3

21 Micha 6:8

We find in Tractate Sotah 4b, "Arrogance is comparable to idolatry" and this is based on Deuteronomy 8:14 which says: "Beware lest your heart grow haughty and you forget the Lord your God. Continuing in Tractate Sotah 5a, it says: "I [God] and a vain person cannot dwell together."

Why are matters of Torah compared to water, as it is written: "Ho, everyone who thirsts, come for water."? [22] This verse comes to tell you: Just as water leaves a high place and flows to a low place, so too, Torah matters are retained only by one whose spirit is lowly, i.e., a humble person." [23]

One of the strongest statements on humility is found in the Midrash *Tanna debei Eliyahu*: "Let everyone be humble with one's parents, teachers, spouse and children, with his whole family near and far, even with the pagan, and so become beloved on high and desirable below."

Maimonides is known for the idea that everything should be in moderation. The exception is humility, to which, since it is so important and fundamental, there is no limit. [24] Ramban (Nahmanides [25]) in a letter to his son, calls humility "the finest of all traits."

"For the end of a mortal is the worm [*the grave*]*."*

"The ignominious end that awaits man's body serves as a most humbling deterrent against delusions of grandeur (Maimonides)." [26]

"If the ultimate destiny of individuals is decay, in the physical sense, then there is nothing one can do to save the physical. Rather, one should emphasize that which is eternal, the soul aspects of human existence. Humility is in order...the obligation of the hour." [27]

4:28 – Envy, lust, and the seeking of honor, drive a person out of the world.

22 Isaiah 55:1
23 Taanit 7a
24 Mishneh Torah, Hilkhot Deot 2:3
25 Spain, d. 1270
26 *Pirkei Avos Treasury*, ArtScroll, p. 227
27 Rabbi Reuven Bulka, p. 147

Here are three personal qualities that have ruined many a human being's life. On the other hand, Rabbi Yosef Marcus [(28)] looks at the other side of the coin, suggesting that though one is born with these three vices, one can choose to sublimate them and use them for holy purposes.

Envy: He can use his envy to be jealous of those who are spiritually superior to him and yearn to become like them.

Lust: He can "lust" for the pleasure of closeness to God. As King David said, "My "soul thirsts for God." [(29)]

Honor: Who is honored? He who honors others. When experienced in a holy way, these three vices remove a person from the physicality of this world and he lives in the atmosphere of the World to Come. [(30)]

Envy or jealousy.

"Envy is rottenness to the bones." [(31)] "A lover of money never has his fill of money, nor a lover of wealth his fill of income." [(32)] The classic example of envy is Korah. [(33)] He and his followers were swallowed alive by the earth.

Lust.

"Starve it and not overindulge [sexual desire, lust] and it is satisfied; however, if one satisfies it [and overindulges] it is starved [and wants more]." [(34)]

Honor.

Honor is legitimate only to enhance respect for Torah and God: [(35)] "The lust for honor is more of an impelling force than all other longings and desires. Were it not for this lust a man would be willing to eat whatever he might get, to wear whatever might cover

28 Pirkei Avot, p. 152

29 Psalms 42:3

30 Based on several sources

31 Proverbs 14:30

32 Ecclesiastes 5:9

33 Numbers 16

34 Tractate 52b

35 Rabbi Yonah Gerondi. *Mesillat Yesharim* by Rabbi Moses Hayyim Luzzatto, d. 1746, Italy

him, and to dwell under whatever roof which might protect him."

Rabbi Tamar Elad-Appelbaum writes: "Multiple forces are in play here: envy (symbolizing the power of the mind), lust (symbolizing the power of the body), and the quest for honor (symbolizing the power of the spirit). And in all these areas, teachers must identify their weaknesses and work on them unceasingly, in order to bequeath this framework for moral living to their children and to their students." (36)

"Jealousy, lust and glory are the roots of most sins." (37)

5:13 – There are four types of human character:

(1) One who says, What is mine is mine, and what is yours is yours, is an average person, though some say this is a Sodom type.

(2) One who says, What is mine is yours and what is yours is mine, is an ignoramus.

(3) One who says, What is mine is yours and what is yours is yours, is pious.

(4) One who says, What is yours is mine and what is mine is mine, is wicked.

The Mishnah evaluates four types of personalities by evaluating their attitude toward their possessions. The bottom line is that the Sages advocate generosity and kindness in all of these matters. Naturally, those who are generous, kind and bighearted are to be preferred. Let's take a brief look at each of the four types.

What is mine is mine, and what is yours is yours, is an average person, though some say this is a Sodom type.

This person's attitude seems to be "each person for him/her self." Not a winning attitude. No wonder that some consider this type as one of Sodom. ("Now the inhabitants of Sodom were very wicked sinner against The Lord". (38) Later, the biblical prophets used the name "Sodom" in a pejorative manner. See Isaiah 1:10, where the prophet chastises corrupt leaders as men of Sodom, and Ezekiel 16:49: "Only this was the sin of your sister Sodom: arrogance!... she did not support the poor and the needy."

36 *Pirkei Avot Lev Shalem,* page 221

37 *Pirkei Avos Treasury,* p. 187

38 Genesis 13:13

One who says, What is mine is yours and what is yours is mine, is an ignoramus.

This type wants to get and not give. A "taker," but not a "giver." This average person will let others give him something, as long as he gets something in return. Nothing remarkable here. No wonder the Sages call this morally unsophisticated person an ignoramus. This system resembles that of communism, which ended in failure.

What is mine is yours and what is yours is yours, is pious.

This person is most admired by the Sages, obviously. He/she is caring, generous and kind. "Kindness is the language which the deaf can hear, the dumb can understand, and the blind can see. The saintly person is constantly engaged in performing benevolent actions and kindly deeds. He dedicates his entire life to the service of God and man. The Hasid is the embodiment of true religion because he inherits in good measure an abundance of God's grace, and lovingkindness." [(39)] This person is not possessive, miserly, or materialistic, as the others. He/she gives freely, but according to the Sages one must not give away more than one fifth of one's possessions. That might put one in a position of needing help from others. The very fact that the Sages put a limit on giving implies that some people had a very generous instinct.

What is yours is mine and what is mine is mine, is wicked.

Such a person is self-centered, and obsessed with his/her possessions.

---

39 Rabbi Shlomo P. Toperoff, *Avot*, p. 314

Prayer

2:18 – "Be mindful in reciting the Shema and the Amidah. When you pray, do not do so as a fixed routine, but as a plea for mercy and grace before God, as it is said, "For God is gracious and compassionate, slow to anger, abounding in kindness…" [1]

Following the destruction of the *Bet Mikdash*, Jews needed a way to be purified from sin. The sacrificial system no longer existed, yet they wanted to be able to connect with God on a regular basis. The rabbis declared that recurrent prayer would suffice. Avodah (worship) would replace animal sacrifice. The Sages called it *Avodah she-ba-lev*, or "the service of the heart."

The earliest structure of daily prayer was based around two parts: the Shema section and the *Amidah* [the "standing" prayer, an essential part of Jewish liturgy]. These two basic components expanded in time to become the contents of the *Siddur*. The Shema [2] was addressed to the Jewish people, acknowledging the oneness and unity of God, and thus the unity of all humanity and all creation. The *Amidah* began as eighteen benedictions, and was later augmented to nineteen. Reciting these two major themes, and the blessings preceding and following, are the core of Jewish worship.

The reference to the Shema includes all three paragraphs, Deuteronomy 6:4-9, 11:13-21, and Numbers 15:37-41. All three paragraphs are designated when "Shema" is mentioned.

While regular recitation of the daily statutory prayers was deemed obligatory, there is always the danger of reciting the words in a mechanical way, making it perfunctory and routine. This Mishnah encourages the worshiper to invest him/herself in a meaningful way when reciting the standard prayers. The Hebrew word for "fixed routine" is "*keva*," and should be balanced with another similar-sounding Hebrew word, "*kavanah*" (intention, meaning). By demanding that prayer not be seen as a burden, to be done with automatically and quickly, but with deep thought and inner spiritual feeling, the worshiper should feel as though he/she

1 Joel 2:13
2 Deuteronomy 6:4-9

is communicating with a God who is "gracious and compassionate, slow to anger and abounding in kindness." This is much different than mumbling some pre-written syllables that one neither understands nor internalizes.

The Hasidic movement put great emphasis on deep spirituality in worship. It should be accompanied by song, dance, merriment, exaltation and an inspired heart. Breslover Hasidim, for example, encourages their followers to meditate in the fields, and speak whatever is in the heart, with words of grace and supplication. They suggest that the ideal time for such meditation and prayer is at night or early in the morning, following or preceding the busy-ness of the day, when all is quiet. Rebbe Nahman, the founder of this school of Hasidism, wrote that it is good to pour out our thoughts before God, like a child pleading before one's father.

The Hasidic Sage, Rabbi Menahem Mendel of Kotzk, was asked by a Polish nobleman: "Why is it that so many of your followers hold you in such high esteem?" He replied: "Because I am able to concentrate on a certain subject of Torah for a very long time."

The most well-known advocate of "*kavanah*" in prayer in modern times is Rabbi Abraham Joshua Heschel,[(3)] himself a scion of a long line of Hasidic masters.

Heschel wrote: "Our goal should be to live life in radical amazement ... Get up in the morning and look at the world in a way that takes nothing for granted. Everything is phenomenal; everything is incredible; never treat life casually. To be spiritual is to be amazed.

"What we lack is not a will to believe but a will to wonder.

"The primary purpose of prayer is not to make requests. The primary purpose is to praise, to sing, to chant. Because the essence of prayer is a song, and man cannot live without a song. Prayer may not save us, but prayer may make us worthy of being saved."

---

3 d. 1972

Reputation

1:13 – A name made great is a name destroyed.

We all know people, personally, or in Hollywood or in the media, who brag and boast of their great achievements. They are usually people of low self-esteem, who are glory-seekers, greedy for honor and fame, exhibitionists, whose only goal is to impress others. Woe unto them, for their efforts inevitably bring them into disgrace and misfortune.

"...a name destroyed...."

In one's quest to make one's name well-known it may happen that in the zest to become famous one may resort to unprincipled means to attain his/her end and thus lose whatever fame and glory acquired.

Scripture teaches us much about obtaining a good name. "A good name is better than fragrant oil", [1] but a good name comes from good deeds and honorable actions, not from self-glorification.

"One's pride will humiliate him, but a humble person will receive honor." [2] Honor comes to one who acts out of a desire to do justice, not to please others or acquire fame.

Kabbalah and Hasidism teach the concept of "*bittul hayesh*" – or total self negation. These philosophies encourage one to be God-centered, not self-centered. Only service to God is worthy of pride: "His heart was proud in the ways of God." [3] It is not self-aggrandizement to be proud in Divine ways.

2:8 – Whoever acquires a good name acquires something for oneself. Whoever acquires for oneself words of Torah acquires for oneself life in the World-to-Come.

Scripture preceded the Mishnah in emphasizing the importance of a positive reputation.

---

1 Ecclesiastes 7:1
2 Proverbs 29:23
3 II Chronicles 17:6

"A good name is rather to be chosen than great riches, and loving favor rather than silver and gold." [4]

This Mishnah, together with 2:8 (above) and 4:17 (below), make very clear the emphasis Judaism places on establishing for oneself a good reputation.

A dear friend of mine, a former congregant, always said that the most important piece of advice he received from his father was to have what he called in Yiddish "*a gutten nomen*," which implies living a life of good deeds, Teshuvah, mitzvot, and studying and living a life of Torah will surely bring one a good name.

"Whoever acquires a good name acquires something for oneself."

Some explain that when a person acquires a positive reputation, he/she should keep it to themselves, quietly and discreetly, unassuming, and not flaunt it.

Another interpretation is that having a good name is like owning a great treasure, but it cannot be transferred to others.

"Whoever acquires for oneself words of Torah acquires for oneself life in the World to Come."

Rabbi Yitz Greenberg comments: "A good name gives a person greater importance in his limited lifetime. Acquiring words and values of Torah brings with it an eternity of goodness and bliss" (p. 82).

Some explain that when one experiences the magnificence of living a life according to Torah values, he/she acquires a taste of *Olam haBa* (the World to Come) in one's present life.

4:17 – There are three crowns: the crown of Torah, the crown of priesthood, and the crown of kingship – but the crown of a good name surpasses them all.

There are many interpretations by commentators regarding this important Mishnah. What is clear, in the end, is that one's reputation can only be earned by each individual. Most commentators agree

4 Proverbs 22:1

that while the first three crowns, Torah, priesthood and royalty, are bestowed upon the owner (even Torah scholarship is reserved with those endowed with a superior intellect), the crown of a good name is attainable by all, and only through acts of righteousness and kindness. The first three crowns are gifts from God, only a good reputation, a good name, one earns for oneself.

The first three crowns, of Torah, priesthood and royalty, are of no value unless connected to a good name. History has shown us that men of scholarship, kohanim and kings, throughout Jewish history, have not always lived up to the high standards of a superior reputation.

"There are three names by which one is called: one that their parents call them, one that other people call them, and one that they earn for themselves. The best of all is the one a person acquires by oneself." [5]

Who is one who deserves a fine name? The Midrash [6] answers that question: "through love, harmony, reverence, companionship, truth, peace, humility, modesty, study, less commerce, service to the scholar, discussions with students, decency, a no that is no and a yes that is yes."

5 Midrash Tanhuma, Parashat Vayakhel, Siman Alef
6 Seder Eliyahu Rabbah 23

Reward and Punishment

1:3 – Do not be like servants who serve their master on condition of receiving a reward.

Jewish tradition is divided on the question whether there is reward and punishment for human actions. The Torah does offer rewards and punishments for various behaviors. The insight that this Mishnah brings is that while one may be rewarded for good actions, behaving in order to be rewarded is not the highest level of morality. Maimonides includes belief in Divine reward and punishment in the eleventh principle of his Thirteen Principles of the Faith.

Even though the idea of reward and punishment is widely accepted, our Mishnah points to a higher level of morality. Rabbi Hertz quotes from Psalms (112:1), "Blessed is the man who fears the Lord, and in His commandments delights greatly." In His commandments, and not in the reward of the commandments, is the Rabbinic comment.

Rabbi Shmuly Yanklowitz brings the insights of the late psychology professor at Harvard University, Lawrence Kohlberg, who is known as a leading expert in moral development. Says Kohlberg there are "six stages of moral development ... In the earliest stages, one is concerned with reward and punishment. In middle stages, one is concerned with adhering to the law and following cultural norms. In the actualized, final stages of moral development, we live by principled conscience and universal ethics. As we mature, our motivations develop toward means that go beyond the personally selfish and toward the (broadly) egalitarian and communal. This is the stage that [this Mishnah] describes here."[(1)]

It is interesting to note the point of view of one of America's great founders, Benjamin Franklin, who wrote in his autobiography: "I never doubted, for instance, the existence of the Deity, that He made the world and governed it by his Providence, that the most acceptable service of God was the doing of good to man, that our

---

1 *Pirkei Avot*, p. 12

souls are immortal, and *that all crime will be punished and virtue rewarded either here or hereafter*" (emphasis added).

Agreeing with the above point of view, Albert Einstein once wrote: "I cannot conceive of a God who rewards and punishes His creations." In this view, the highest reward one can receive is service to God, doing an act which the Sages call acting "*le-shem shamayim* – for the sake of Heaven." Another phrase used by the Sages to refer to doing something for its own reward is doing an act "*lishmah* – for its own sake."

The Mishnah is teaching that God is not a "Divine bellhop" who dishes out prizes for those who follow the rules. As Rabbi Abraham J. Twerski phrases the matter, "It should be apparent that reward and punishment are essentially juvenile motivations." (2) The highest motivation is love of God.

See also the chapter on Mitzvot, especially 4:2.

2 *Visions of the Fathers*, p. 21

Self-Esteem

1:14 – If I am not for myself, who will be for me?

See the section on this Mishnah under the chapter "Particularism vs. Universalism." There I have dealt with this Mishnah in detail, and much of it relates to the issue of self-esteem.

2:18 – Do not be wicked in your own eyes.

This section of Mishnah 2:18 deals with a specific part of self-esteem. Self-esteem is the feeling and opinion one has of oneself. The Sages were far ahead of their time in believing that a healthy person must have a strong sense of self, as expressed in 1:14. The flip side of that idea is that one must not have a negative self-image. In item (b) below, I bring the wise views of Rabbi Abraham J. Twerski, who is not only a distinguished rabbinic scholar, but also a well-known and highly respected psychiatrist.

Rabbi Dr. Twerski writes, in his commentary on Pirkei Avot: [1] "In psychology we distinguish between *guilt* and *shame*. Guilt is a distressful sensation resulting from the awareness that one has done something wrong. Healthy guilt can lead to *teshuvah*, to making amends for the wrong and to take preventive measures to avoid a recurrence. Shame, on the other hand, is a sensation that one is somehow bad, even though one may not be able to identify why he should think of himself as being bad. To put it another way, guilt is a statement, 'I made a mistake,' whereas shame is a statement, 'I *am* a mistake.' In the latter case, no corrective action can be taken, since one has no idea of what must be corrected."

The Talmud makes a wise observation. [2] "A person should view oneself as though he were exactly half-righteous and half-wicked. In other words, he should act as though the plates of his scale are balanced, so that if he performs one mitzvah, he is fortunate, as he tilts his balance to the scale of merit. If he transgresses one prohibition, woe to him, as he tilts his balance to the scale of being

---

1 *Visions of the Fathers,* p. 130

2 Tractate Kiddushin 40b

wicked, as it is stated: "But one sin destroys much good,"[3] which means that due to one sin that a person transgresses he squanders much good." Thus by seeing oneself as wicked, he can fall into despair and then lose hope of doing good, and become more and more wicked. This Talmudic statement may be the source of Maimonides' view that one should not see oneself as totally wicked and incorrigible, because then one will give up and will not repent.

"If one considers oneself wicked, he/she will become depressed and will not be able to serve God joyfully and with a contented heart."[4]

Several Hasidic masters were concerned enough about a person's self-esteem that they coined well-used aphorisms. The most famous is that of Rabbi Simcha Bunam of Pshis'cha: "Every person should have two pockets. In one should be a piece of paper on which is written: 'I am but dust and ashes.'[5] In the other: 'For my sake was the world created.'"[6]

Another aphorism is by Rabbi Menahem Mendel of Kotzk: "Not only is one who hates another soul called wicked – but someone who hates oneself is also called wicked."

A third aphorism is by Rabbi Yaakov Yosef of Polnoye: "If one does not recognize one's own worth, how can one appreciate the worth of another?"[7]

There is an oft-told case in the Talmud taught by the famed Rabbi Akiva: "Two people who were walking in the desert, but only one of them had a flask of water; if both of them would drink from it, they would both die [there is not enough water]. If only one drinks from it, he would live. What should be done? Rabbi Akiva taught: Your life (i.e. the life of the one who owns the flask) comes before the life of your fellow."[8]

Is it not selfish to put yourself ahead of another? Rabbi Akiva

---

3 Ecclesiastes 9:18

4 *Tanya*, chapter one. (The *Tanya* is a book of Hasidic philosophy, by Rabbi Shneur Zalman of Liadi, the founder of Chabad Hasidism, first published in 1797.)

5 Genesis 18:27

6 Tractate Sanhedrin 37a

7 All three of these maxims can be found in *Hasidic Wisdom*, by Simcha Raz

8 Tractate Bava Metzia 62a

taught that the mitzvah, "Love your neighbor as yourself" [9] is a cardinal principle in the Torah. [10] Implied in that mitzvah from the Torah is the idea that one must love oneself in order to love others. In other words, Love your neighbor as you love yourself. If you do not love yourself, how can you love someone else?

The philosopher and essayist, Ahad Ha'am [11] wrote that the advice not to appear to be wicked in one's own eyes, applies not only to individuals but to nations as well. He wrote: "Nothing is more dangerous for a nation or for an individual than to plead guilty to imaginary sins. Where the sin is real – by honest endeavor the sinner can purify himself. But when one has been persuaded to suspect himself unjustly – what can he do? Our greatest need is emancipation from self-contempt." Ahad Ha'am had in mind the dangerous appearance of self-hatred among Jews in nineteenth century Europe, due to some Jews internalizing the hatred of the gentile world and widespread antisemitism.

An old weaver in Edinburgh prayed each Sunday, "Lord, grant me a high opinion of myself." A worthy prayer, indeed!

There is a wealth of ideas in the several books I have edited and written as a result of my doctoral dissertation on self-esteem, including *Glad To Be Me, Teaching People to Love Themselves*, and *Self-Concept Sourcebook.*

---

9 Leviticus 19:18

10 Genesis Rabbah 24:7

11 Pen name for Asher Ginsberg, born near Kiev 1856, died in Tel Aviv 1927

Speech and Silence

1:17 – All my life I grew up among Sages and I found that nothing is better for a person than silence.... And one who talks too much causes sin.

Silence as a spiritual tool is greatly appreciated in biblical and post-biblical literature.

"Even a fool, if he keeps silent, is deemed wise; intelligent, if he seals his lips." [(1)]

The Talmud teaches: [(2)] "What is the meaning of that which is written: 'For You silence is praise'? [(3)] The best remedy of all is silence, i.e., the optimum form of praising God is silence. In the Land of Israel they have an adage: If a word is worth one coin, silence is worth two."

Rabbi Marc D. Angel and Rabbi Jonathan Sacks commenting on this Mishnah, explain: "A rabbinic teaching claims that the Torah has seventy 'faces,' i.e., can be interpreted in a variety of ways. A Hasidic rabbi taught that one of the seventy 'faces' is silence." [(4)]

Professor Michael Fishbane of the University of Chicago, wrote: "There are two kinds of silence. One of these is natural silence, and is characterized by the absence of noise. It is ...negative silence. The other kind of silence is spiritual. With respect to deliberate speech, silence conveys the ethical potential of words. Prayer may also stand at this juncture of silence and speech." [(5)]

Some of the most important moments in Jewish history occurred when the world was silent. The Torah was given in silence on Mt. Sinai: "No bird sang or flew, the sea did not roar, no ox lowed, no creature spoke, the world was silent and still." [(6)]

When Aaron's two sons die, Moses offers a few words of comfort, [(7)] but Aaron could do no more than sit in silence. Aaron

1 Proverbs 17:28
2 Tractate Megillah 18a
3 Psalms 65:2
4 *The Koren Pirkei Avot,* p. 24
5 *Sacred Attunement: A Jewish Theology,* p. 13
6 Exodus Rabbah 29
7 Lev. 10:3

is speechless. No words are adequate to express his grief. *Vayidom Aaron!* ["And Aaron was silent"]. In two Hebrew words the Torah describes the powerful emotional reaction that seized Aaron in this terrible and trying moment in his life.

When Elijah fled for his life, running away from King Ahab and his wife Jezebel to the Sinai desert, and the Lord passed by, "and a great strong wind tore into the mountains and broke the rocks in pieces before the Lord, but the Lord was not in the earthquake; and after the earthquake a fire, but the Lord was not in the fire; and after the fire a soft, quiet sound." (8)

Rabbi Reuven P. Bulka comments: "One who is busy talking has no time for doing, and one who is busy doing has no time or need for talking." (9)

Jewish mystics cherished moments of silence more than most people. Rabbi Nahman of Breslov (10) taught that every human being must have at least an hour every day to be alone in silence. He also said: "As children we learn to speak; as elders we learn silence. And this is the great flaw we have: that we learn to speak before we learn to be quiet."

Some mystics observed a "*ta-anit dibbur* – fast of silence," instead of a fast from food, realizing that a fast of silence is a better way to do Teshuvah (repentance) than a fasting from food. (11)

Even Shakespeare, the great artist and master wordsmith, acknowledged the superiority of silence over words when he wrote: "Silence is the most perfect herald of joy. I were but little happy if I could say how much." (12)

In Israel, silence is one of the premier methods of honoring martyrs of past history. During Yom HaShoah and Yom HaZikaron (memorializing those who died in Israel's wars), there is a two-minute period of silence when the entire country stands at silent attention. A siren blasts throughout the country at a pre-determined hour, and even those in their automobiles stop, get out of their cars, and stand at attention.

---

8 I Kings 19:11-13

9 *As A Tree By the Waters*, p. 46

10 Ukraine, d. 1810

11 Hafetz Hayim, Mishnah Berurah 571:2

12 *Much Ado About Nothing*

A rabbinic colleague told the story about a visit to Israel when he led a pilgrimage of members of his congregation. He tells of his colorful and loquacious guide. Like all of Israel's guides, he was knowledgeable, entertaining, and full of stories and history.

Israel's well-trained tour guides are intelligent and articulate; talkative and glib. During this particular tour, the guide was especially gifted in his ability to describe the sites and scenes of the State of Israel. He lectured to the group on history, philosophy, geography, archeology, economics, politics and military strategy.

When the group arrived at the *Kotel* (the Western Wall), however, he led them out of the bus, and remained standing in the back without uttering a word. During the entire stay at the *Kotel*, not a word from this normally talkative teacher.

When everyone returned to the bus, the rabbi asked him about this unusual behavior. The guide replied: "At the special training school for guides we are repeatedly warned not to say anything at the Western Wall. At the *Kotel*, he said, with obvious emotion, the tourist must listen not to the guide's voice but to higher voices, to greater voices, to the voice of Jewish history, to the 'still small voice' of God."

In a wonderful book of advice, [13] Kent Nerburn writes about silence and solitude:

> "It is worth the struggle. Slowly, inexorably, we emerge into the ultimate quiet of solitude.
>
> "We are in a place where we are beyond thoughts – where we hear each sound and feel each heartbeat; where we are present to each change of sunlight on the earth around us, and we live in the awareness of the ongoing presence of life.
>
> "In this awareness the whole world changes around us. A tree ceases to be an object and becomes a living thing. We can smell its richness, hear its rustlings, sense its rhythms. Silence becomes a symphony. Time changes from a series of moments strung together to a seamless motion riding on the rhythms of the stars.
>
> "Solitude is a place you reach, not a decision you make."

---

13 *Letters To My Son,* New World Library, 1993

"And one who talks too much causes sin."

Those who are loquacious are more likely to gossip and slander. Role modeling good behavior is far superior to long speeches in influencing others. The Sages taught often about the evils of "*leshon ha'ra,)* (gossip). They taught that *leshon ha'ra* is worse than murder, since it affects three people, the one who speaks it, the one who hears it, and the one about whom it is told. [(14)]

Some understand this part of the Mishnah, "talking too much and causing sin," as a criticism of those who are eloquent but do not follow through on their spoken words.

The biblical prophet said it many centuries ago: [(15)]

> "The Lord is in the Holy Temple. Let all the earth keep silence in God's Presence!"

2:5 – Do not say anything that cannot be understood at once in the hope that it will eventually be understood.

This part of our Mishnah lends itself to several interpretations. Most commentators explain it to mean that a teacher should make certain that he is clear, to be sure that what he is teaching is understood, and not to assume that eventually what he is teaching will become clear in the minds of the students.

Rabbi Joseph Hertz offers an alternate possible explanation: "Divulge not things that ought to be kept secret, on the plea that in the end all things are sure to become public knowledge." [(16)]

Rabbi Yitz Greenberg further elucidates: "Brilliant original, and complex ideas can be stated with clarity, precision, and focus so that people will understand them." [(17)]

---

14 Numbers Rabbah 19:2

15 Habakkuk 2:20

16 *Sayings of the Fathers,* p. 32

17 *Sage Advice,* p. 77

Tzedakah (Charity)

5:15 – There are four types of donor to charity:

1) One who wishes to give but does not want others to give, begrudges others.

2) One who wants others to give but does not himself give, begrudges himself.

3) One who gives and wants others to give is pious.

4) One who does not himself give and does not want others to give is wicked.

Of the four types of charity donors, the one whom the Sages call "pious" ("Hasid"), is one who not only contributes himself, but also encourages others to give. The Talmud further teaches that one who causes others to perform a mitzvah is greater than one who does a mitzvah oneself. (1)

The Talmud has many things to teach about the importance of giving tzedakah. For example: Rav Asi teaches that the commandment to give charity is considered equivalent to all of the other mitzvot in the Torah. (2) Further: Someone who gives charity in secret (*tzedakah be-seter*) is greater than Moses. (3) (See Proverbs 21:14: "A gift given in secret soothes anger"). And: Someone who gives a coin to a poor person receives six blessings, while someone who consoles him with words of comfort and encouragement receives eleven blessings. (4)

Even the poor must give tzedakah. (5)

One of the most oft-quoted statements about tzedakah in the Talmud is that a person's character can be judged by these three qualities (notice the alliteration in Hebrew: *koso, keeso, v'ka'aso*): *koso*, his cup, how he acts after drinking; *keeso*, his wallet, how he conducts his business and how charitable he is; and *kaaso*, his

1 Tractate Bava Metzia 9a
2 Tractate Bava Batra 9a
3 Tractate Bava Batra 9b
4 Ibid
5 Tractate Gittin 7b

anger, how he controls his temper. [6]

In Maimonides' Golden Ladder of Tzedakah, the highest level is the person who helps a poor individual by giving him a loan to help him start his own business, helping to maintain his self-respect.

How do we know if a beggar requesting charity is truly poor? Rabbi Hayyim of Tsanz [7] had this to say about fraudulent charity collectors: "The merit of charity is so great that I am happy to give to 100 beggars even if only one might actually be needy. Some people, however, act as if they are exempt from giving charity to 100 beggars in the event that one might be a fraud." [8]

There is a well-known story of a great Sage who was a close confidant of one of the sultans in the Middle Ages. His enemies' plots against him always failed because he enjoyed the sultan's trust and admiration. His detractors would not give up, though. Finally they approached the sultan and told him that the rabbi was hiding some of his income to avoid taxes. When the sultan approached the Sage and asked him the total value of his fortune, the number he gave was considerably less than what the records showed he actually possessed. The sultan, in anger, had him thrown into prison for misrepresenting his financial information.

The sultan could not comprehend why the rabbi, a man of great integrity, would misrepresent his wealth. He visited the rabbi in prison to ask him about this. The rabbi's response was: "I told you how much I gave to charity because that is the one thing that I truly possess and no one can take it away from me. As you may see, the rest of my fortune has been taken away from me and I no longer in possess it. But, the *tzedakah* that I gave is mine forever!"

The story echoes a statement in the Talmud [9] by the righteous King Munbaz who lived at the end of the Second Temple era. His critics accused him of squandering his treasures and those of his ancestors. One of his retorts was:

> "My fathers hoarded for others, but I have hoarded for myself, as it is stated, 'and for you it will be charity.'"

The simple understanding of Munbaz' words was that by

6 Tractate Eruvin 65a

7 Poland, d. 1876

8 From Arthur Kurzweil

9 Tractate Bava Batra 11a

giving tzedakah he was generating reward for himself in the next world. However, that would have been redundant because Munbaz had already stated earlier that his tzedakah was generating reward for the next world. A deeper understanding of his response then is that tzedakah actually renders that money as your own possession in the here and now.

These stories convey a profound message: that which you give away is truly your possession. Everything else is ephemeral and can be here one day and gone the next. [(10)]

This story by an anonymous author is a good example of the importance of tzedakah in Jewish life: A man went to his physician to complain about his heart. The physician told him to stretch out his hand so that he might feel his pulse.

"But Doctor," said the patient, "it is my heart I am complaining about."

"I know," said the physician, "but from your hand and its pulse I can tell you about your heart."

The soundness of a Jew's heart can be judged from his hand. When the pulse of tzedakah does not beat strongly in the life of the Jew, it indicates a weakening of his total Jewish commitment.

The following story illustrates perhaps more than anything else, the high priority given to tzedakah in Jewish life in previous generations. [(11)]

Check Out My Room

A prominent rabbi of Newton, Mass., attended a housewarming party at a large, beautiful home in his wealthy Boston suburban community.

Guests flurried to and fro checking out every unusual piece of furniture, every exotic light fixture, every foreign imported piece of hand-crafted art, thick azure carpets, golden hand-carved door handles both inside and outside, and on and on and on.

During the course of the evening, the owners related to their guests that they had paid the highest fee for their interior decorator, but it was worth every penny. The results were astonishing. Every

10 From Chabad of the West Side [of New York]

11 Included in my book, *Jewish Stories from Heaven and Earth,* p. 194

decision, down to the last window treatment, was just impeccable.

They could not have been more pleased.

"This," they declared, in contrast to what most people thought, was how a home should be furnished, "was interior decorating."

About an hour passed and the elderly mother of the hostess, who lived with her daughter and son-in-law, asked her rabbi friend to come upstairs and take a look at her room.

Having left the posh living room and dining room of this large, magnificently appointed, wealthy and lavish suburban home, the elderly woman opened the door of her upstairs bedroom and pointed her finger toward the window sill. When the Rabbi looked, he was astounded at what he saw.

The woman did not point, as her daughter did, to any of the furniture or decorations in the room. She pointed only to the window sill, toward a row of charity boxes, what is called in Yiddish "pushkes," – one for every worthwhile cause imaginable, – hospitals, *yeshivot* [religious schools], orphanages, battered women's shelters, homes for children who were blind or deaf, funds for the handicapped – you name it! One for every single Jewish institution in the world that she could find, which distributed charity boxes for people to drop coins and return when full.

Before the modern methods of fund-raising large sums, these small charity boxes "decorated" kitchen windows in every traditional Jewish home.

"Now, Rabbi," said the elderly woman, gazing proudly at her window sill filled with charity boxes – "*this* is interior decorating!"

Wise People and Their Wisdom

1:11 – Sages, be careful in what you say, lest you incur the penalty of exile and find yourself banished to a place of evil waters, where your disciples who follow you may drink from them and die, with the result that the name of Heaven will be profaned.

This Mishnah cautions scholars and others about the positive and negative power of words. As written above, the wise Hasidic master, Rabbi Menahem Mendel of Kotzk taught that "Not everything that one thinks is fit to say; not everything that one says is fit to write; not everything that one writes is fit to publish." If this is true of scholars, how much more so does it apply to average people. Once words are uttered, they are not easy to take back. Our Mishnah applies to all scholars, all people in authority, and every living person.

The Talmud gives the following example: "One should always be careful in wording one's replies, since on the basis of the answer which Aaron said to Moses, the heretics were able to deny God, as Scripture states, 'And I cast it into the fire and this calf came out.'[(1)] Aaron's words almost admit that the golden calf had Divine powers."[(2)]

"Lest you incur the penalty of exile and find yourself banished to a place of evil waters…."

Evil waters in rabbinic terminology is a euphemism for heresy. In Roman times, there were many reasons for the Sages to be cautious about the dangers of heresy. "A Torah scholar who lacks wisdom is worse than an offensive carcass."[(3)] Rabbi Joseph Hertz explains the historical background: The author of this Mishnah "had witnessed the persecution of the religious teachers under King Alexander Jannai and during the fratricidal conflict of his successors. Many of the teachers had suffered death, others had to flee for their lives into distant lands. In such a time – [the author] guardedly warns the contemporary teachers of Judaism – the wise are circumspect

1 Exodus 32:24
2 Tractate Megillah 25b
3 Midrash Vayikra Rabbah 1:15

in their utterances on public questions. Aside from the peril to their persons, there was real danger to the faith. Several of the Sages had fled to Alexandria, the then capital of the intellectual world, and seething with schools of fantastic speculation. The disciples of those exiled Sages followed them to Alexandria; and there they found a Jewry that had discarded the Hebrew language, and held the observances and institutions of the Torah to be mere symbols and allegories.

Many of these disciples succumbed to this Hellenistic Judaism which left its followers nothing to live by, and nothing to die for. To the pious Palestinian Jew, Alexandria was indeed 'a place of evil waters,' a fountain of heresy." [(4)]

Dr. William Berkson teaches: "That errors in philosophy and law can indeed have grave consequences may be seen in the 20th century, when the adoption of Nazism and Bolshevism led to the suffering and death of millions of people. Ideas have consequences." [(5)]

Abravanel comments that teachers must be careful when teaching mystical secrets of the Torah, especially to students who are not on a high enough level to understand such matters. This may be dangerous for them, and have a negative influence on them.

Some interpret this Mishnah as relating to Jews who may consider unfair dealings with gentiles, and who then have disdain for the Torah and the Jewish tradition.

"Sages, be careful in what you say, lest you incur the penalty of exile and find yourself banished to a place of evil waters..."

Being careless with one's teaching may push oneself over a red line and encourage a teacher to go "off the derekh," i.e., become extreme or heretical, and bring spiritual death.

"With the result that the name of Heaven will be profaned."

This may mean that scholars should live up to their own words before they ask others to do so. Role models who fail may cause followers to lose their respect for them and for the Torah and mitzvot and thus blasphemy occurs.

In the modern age it is particularly important to use words

4 Pages 21-22
5 P. 36

carefully, since modern technology (internet, social media, etc.) makes it possible for one's words to go viral and circulate all over the world instantaneously, unless one exercises extreme attentiveness in use of words. Several world leaders have misspoken on an "open microphone," without realizing that their words were being heard, and supposedly confidential comments were thus disseminated throughout the world.

Women

1:5 – Do not gossip inordinately with women. This was said about one's own wife; all the more so does it apply to another man's wife. Hence the Sages say: a man who talks too much with a woman brings trouble on himself, neglects the study of Torah, and in the end will inherit Gehinnom.

Many traditional commentators emphasize two things regarding this Mishnah. One, that is does not, in general, comply with the overall positive opinion of women in the Talmud (see quotations following). Two, that in the days of the Sages, women's place was obviously much different than in modern times, and what the Mishnah is saying is that idle chatter may lead to possibilities of immoral conduct.

A full treatment of the issues involved is very well laid out in the commentary of Rabbi Shmuly Yanklowitz. [(1)]

Rabbi Reuven Bulka comments: "In this distorted perception of women, the ultimate loser is man. It is he who *causes harm to himself*, in that by disparaging his partner he thereby disparages himself, and begins a dangerous dehumanizing process. The partner is seen as a thing rather than a being, the depersonalization of the partner eventually depersonalizes the husband, who, in this distorted worldview, will become alienated from all meaningful endeavor, will *desist from Torah study*, and shrink away spiritually."

The very wise and always relevant views of Rabbi Irving (Yitz) Greenberg are most welcome in this controversial evaluation of the role of women. "In a society where men and women were socially isolated from each other (and women were often segregated in their own homes), excessive socializing and talk between men and women could lead to improper thoughts and actions. This passage is a reminder of the extraordinary entrance of women into contemporary society and their rise to the dignity of public activity in the past century. It is not that there are no sexual and relational moral risks in the increased interaction between men and women. But the religious emphasis has shifted to women acting and leading

1 *Pirkei Avot,* pages 18-21

in the public sphere as full participants rather than women staying home to preserve their modesty as well as that of the men. In other words, nowadays, self-control in each other's presence rather than social segregation is the key to upholding morality and modesty."[2]

There is no doubt that classical rabbinical literature includes statements that are both laudatory and derogatory of women. A sample of the laudatory statements: A man without a wife lives without joy, blessing, and good; a man should love his wife as himself and respect her more than himself. [3]

Women have greater faith than men. [4]

Israel was redeemed from Egypt by virtue of its righteous women. [5]

2:8 – "The more wives, the more witchcraft. The more maidservants, the more lewdness."

Rival wives resort to witchcraft to get the attention and affection of their husband. There is no record of Talmudic Sages having more than one wife at a time. Rabbenu Gershom [6] made an edict for Ashkenazi Jews not permitting more than one wife at a time, a revolutionary ruling.

"The more maidservants, the more lewdness..."

Maidservants typically had a low standard of moral behavior, and this was hence discouraged.

2 *Sage Advice*, p. 24
3 Tractate Yevamot 62b
4 Midrash Sifre 133
5 Tractate Sota 11b
6 b. 960 CE, France, d. 1040, Germany

World Ethics

1:2: On three things the world exists: on the Torah, on Divine worship, and on acts of loving kindness.

These three pillars are the essential ingredients for a rich, meaningful and satisfying life. Let us focus for now on the third of the three pillars (other comments on study of Torah and prayer can be found in other parts of this commentary). The basis of acts of loving kindness is scattered all through Scripture and rabbinic literature. We will share some of these valuable and significant aphorisms below.

Of primary and critical importance is this verse in Psalms (89:3): "The world is built on loving kindness." The prophet Micah's words resound throughout history and literature (6:8): "God has told you, O mortal, what is good, and what The Lord requires of you: Only to do justice, to love kindness, and to walk humbly with your God."

In the early part of a Jewish prayer book (*siddur*) this quotation from the Mishnah is often found: "These are the things that have no definite quantity: The corners of the field, first-fruits; the offerings brought on appearing at the Temple on the three pilgrimage festivals, the performance of acts of kindness; and the study of the Torah. The following are the things for which one enjoys the fruits in this world while the principal remains in the world to come: Honoring one's father and mother; the performance of acts of kindness; and the making of peace between a person and his friend; and the study of the Torah is equal to them all." (1)

"The Sages taught that acts of kindness are superior to charity in three respects: Charity can be performed only with one's money, while acts of kindness can be performed both with his person and with his money. Charity is given to the poor, while acts of kindness are performed both for the poor and for the rich. Charity is given to the living, while acts of kindness are performed both for the living and for the dead." (2)

"There are three distinguishing marks of the Jewish people. They

1 Mishnah Tractate Peah 1:1
2 Tractate Sukkah 49b

are merciful, they are modest, and they perform acts of kindness."[3]

Once, Rabban Yohanan ben Zakkai left Jerusalem and Rabbi Yehoshua followed after him. And he saw the Holy Temple destroyed. Rabbi Yehoshua said: Woe to us, for this is destroyed – the place where all of Israel's sins are forgiven, i.e., *by bringing of sacrifices.* Rabbi Yohanan said to him: My son, do not be distressed, for we have a form of atonement just like it. And what is it? Acts of kindness, as it says,[4] "For I desire kindness, not sacrifice."[5]

"Whoever denies the centrality of acts of lovingkindness, it is as if such a one has denied God (*kofer be-ikkar*)."[6]

Jews should imitate the ways of God *(imitatio Dei*): "One should follow the attributes of the Blessed Holy One. He provides several examples.

Just as God clothes the naked, as it is written: "And the Lord God made for Adam and for his wife garments of skin, and clothed them,"[7] so too, should you clothe the naked.

Just as the Blessed Holy One, visits the sick, as it is written with regard to God's appearing to Abraham following his circumcision: "And the Lord appeared unto him by the terebinths of Mamre,"[8] so too, should you visit the sick.

Just as the Blessed Holy One consoles mourners, as it is written: "And it came to pass after the death of Abraham, that God blessed Isaac his son,"[9] so too, should you console mourners.

Just as the Blessed Holy One buried the dead, as it is written: "And he was buried in the valley in the land of Moab,"[10] so too, should you bury the dead."[11]

The Torah begins and ends with acts of kindness: "Its beginning is an act of kindness, as it is written: "And the Lord God made for Adam and for his wife garments of skin, and clothed them."[12] And

---

3 Tractate Yevamot 79a

4 Hosea 6:6

5 *Avot deRabbi Natan* 4:5

6 Midrash Kohelet Rabbah 7

7 Genesis 3:21

8 Genesis 18:1

9 Genesis 25:11

10 Deuteronomy 34:6

11 Tractate Sota 14a

12 Genesis 3:21

its end is an act of kindness, as it is written: "And he was buried in the valley in the land of Moab."[(13)]

"Someone who gives a coin to a poor person receives six blessings, while someone who consoles him with words of comfort and encouragement receives eleven blessings."[(14)]

"God says: the acts of kindness that you do for each other are more precious to Me than all the thousand sacrifices which King Solomon brought before Me."[(15)] And Hosea 6:6 says: "For I desire kindness, not sacrifice".

"Acts of kindness" in Hebrew is "*Gemilut Hasadim.*" The Hebrew acronym for these two words is "*Gemach,*" and there are "*Gemach*" societies in most Jewish communities that provide free loans, free Jewish burial, used clothing, and many other free services, as "acts of kindness."

When Rabbi Chaim Soloveitchik, the well-known intellectual giant of Brisk, Poland[(16)] was nearing death, he resisted having several epithets engraved on his tombstone. He did not want to be called *gaon* (Torah genius), or "Rabbi" or "Sage of the Jewish community." The only words he wanted on the tombstone were *rav hesed*, great in kindness. To this world-renowned scholar, the greatness of one's intellectual abilities and Talmudic scholarship were not as important as *hesed*, his exhibition of kindness and mercy during his lifetime.

2:1 – Reflect on three things and you will not fall into transgression: know what is above you: a seeing eye, a hearing ear, and a book in which all your deeds are written.

The Sages differ on the question as whether God controls our actions, and whether God allows free will. What they did not disagree about is that there is a God who is aware of our deeds. This Mishnah makes clear the rabbinic view that while God gives us free will to do good or evil, God knows what we do, and, metaphorically, God sees and hears all that we do, and that all our

13 Deuteronomy 34:6; Tractate Sota 14a

14 Tractate Bava Batra 9b

15 Yalkut Shimoni on Hosea No. 522

16 d. 1918

deeds are recorded in a metaphorical book. This is apparently the same metaphorical book mentioned in the High Holiday prayer book (*Mahzor*), referred to as "*Sefer Ha Zikhronot* –The Book of Remembrance." In other words, God sees all, hears all, and records all. These three aspects of Divine awareness are, in the view of the Sages, deterrents to sin. The net result is not different from the admonition in Avot 3:1.

The basic lesson is this: "When people feel that they are being watched, they tend to behave more admirably." [(17)]

2:6 – In a place where there are no men, you be a man.

The word "man," as in Yiddish "*mensch*," implies a person who is a worthy, mature person.

As with several teachings in Pirkei Avot, and other parts of the Mishnah and the Gemara, there are often many possible interpretations. The simplest and clearest explanation of this Mishnah is that one should step up to the plate when there are no others assuming a position of leadership. This is an important teaching, and thus often quoted.

How many times in history did one person rise up and become a leader when circumstances required, and bring salvation when no one else had the courage or confidence to do so? In modern times we think of the Righteous Gentiles who risked their lives to save Jews during World War II. How many more Jewish lives could have been saved if there were more such people, brave and valiant, who defied the Nazi establishment and jeopardized their own safety because it was the just and moral way and time to act? While Raoul Wallenberg, Oscar Schindler, Chiune Sugihara are obviously among the best well-known, there were many, many others who made the courageous leap to act like a "mensch" when the opportunity arose.

Leviticus 19:16 admonishes: "Do not stand idly by the blood of your neighbor." One 18th century Sephardic commentary, the *Me'am Lo'ez*, written by Rabbi Yitzchak Magriso, writes: "Included in the commandment, 'Do not stand idly by the blood of your neighbor' is an injunction that if one sees his neighbor in danger

---

17 *Koren Pirkei Avot,* p. 30

and has the ability to do something, he must do everything in his power to help him."

Rabbi Dorothy A. Richman writes on this verse: "One afternoon during an Introduction to Jewish Philosophy class, my professor posed the following question: If you are walking by a swimming pool, and you see someone drowning, what is your obligation to intervene? Must you dive in? Call for help? Throw her a line?

"According to American law, there is no legal obligation to rescue a person in danger. Jewish law, however, provides a different answer. The duty to positively act to save a life comes in this week's Torah portion: "Do not stand idly by the blood of your neighbor." [18] Commenting on this verse, the Talmud specifically addresses the question raised by my professor: [19]

"'Whence do we know that if a man sees his fellow drowning, mauled by beasts, or attacked by robbers, he is bound to save him? From the verse, "You shall not stand by the blood of your neighbor!"'"

"All of the situations raised by the Talmud pose potential danger to the rescuer, yet we are still commanded to act. The Talmud goes on to discuss the extent of this obligation – explaining that this Biblical command requires Jews to expend up to all of their resources, financial and physical, to save human life.

"Elie Wiesel, speaking at the Darfur Emergency Summit in July 2004, interpreted the ancient verse to highlight its contemporary global implications:

"*Lo ta'amod al dam re'echa* is a Biblical commandment. Thou shall not stand idly by the shedding of the blood of thy fellow man. The word is not *achi'cha*, thy Jewish brother, but *re'echa*, thy fellow human being, be he or she Jewish or not. All are entitled to live with dignity and hope. All are entitled to live without fear and pain." [20]

Rabbi Yonah Gerondi [21] comments: Do not be overly humble and tell yourself, I am not capable of acting, so I will just sit and do nothing.

---

18 Leviticus 19:16

19 Sanhedrin 73a

20 My Jewish Learning on Parashat Aharei Mot

21 Spain, d. 1263

Others comment: Even if you are the only person doing the right thing, you must not follow the crowd and do nothing. Step up and act. Be a mensch!

In the Torah, our father Abraham is called an *Ivri* (a Hebrew). *Ivri* is related to the Hebrew "*ever*," "side." The Midrash[22] explains that Abraham was on one side, believing in one God, and the rest of the world were on the other side, i.e. pagans.

As descendants of Abraham, Jews should always be prepared to stand against the rest of the world when necessary, rising up for a moral cause.

Maimonides comments: If you live in a community where there are no wise leaders, you must be your own teacher, your own source of inspiration. In other words, where there are no leaders, you make yourself a leader.

Rabbi Berel Wein writes: "Sodom was destroyed not because of its hordes of evildoers, but because it lacked ten good people in its midst. Our task, therefore, is to be a good person, no matter how lonely such a policy may be. If there are no others, then the responsibility upon us to be 'the leader' is even greater. Complacency, defeatism, depression, inaction, and passive acceptance of evil people and ideas, are all foreign to Judaism."[23]

Others explain: Even when there is no one nearby, be a mensch. Do not act one way, morally, when people are watching, and another way (immorally) when no one is watching.

Another interpretation: The opposite is also true. If there are others who are leading, do not act aggressively and push yourself into a position of leadership.

Rabbi Marc D. Angel[24] writes:

Stand Up, Stand Tall

"And the Lord said unto Moses: Rise up early in the morning and stand [tall] before Pharaoh..."[25]

22 Genesis Rabbah 42:8
23 *Pirkei Avos*, p. 70
24 New York, b. 1945
25 Shemoth 9:13

Rabbi Hayyim Benattar, author of the *Ohr haHayyim* commentary on Torah, comments on this verse that God instructed Moses – a naturally humble man – to stand tall, not to bend his head in the presence of Pharaoh. Moses was not to think of himself as being subservient to Pharaoh; on the contrary, Moses was to consider himself to be Pharaoh's superior. Moses was coming at the behest of God; Moses was representing justice and morality. Although Moses was to retain inner humility, he was not to show deference to the wicked Pharaoh.

Often enough, people are confronted with wickedness and injustice; but instead of standing tall in opposition to the perpetrators of evil, people bow their heads. They lose self-confidence. They think: I am too small and too weak to resist. It's best to go along or to stay quiet. Resistance can be unpleasant, even dangerous. Thus, evil continues to spread.

God's command to Moses to stand tall before Pharaoh should be construed as a command to each of us to stand tall in opposition to tyrants, manipulators, liars, and agents of corruption of all kinds. While retaining our inner humility and gentleness, we must not bend our heads in the presence of wicked and unjust people. To show subservience is to give the forces of evil another victory over goodness and truth.

The late Professor Norman Geras, who taught at the University of Manchester in England, wrote about "the contract of mutual indifference." His basic thesis was that when people become indifferent to the injustices perpetrated against others, the general morality of society declines. If we don't care about the sufferings of others, we cannot expect them to care about our sufferings. If we look aside when others are being abused, we cannot expect them to stand up for us when we are the victims of abuse. Mutual indifference is the sign of a morally defective society/world. It is not only degrading to the victims of injustice; it is degrading to the perpetrators themselves. It robs everyone of their essential humanity.

Professor Geras writes: "To accept the world as it is (more or less), is to help to prolong a state of grave danger. This world, accommodating and countenancing too much of what ought not to be tolerated – plain persistent injustice, stark avoidable human suffering – is a world very receptive to present and future atrocity, a world overpopulated with bystanders. As long as the situation lasts, it degrades the moral culture of the planet. It poisons the conscience of humankind." [26]

How can the contract of mutual indifference be rectified? How can humanity overcome widespread apathy in the face of injustice? How can the arrogant be humbled and the wicked be foiled? There is only one answer, and it is for each person to assume personal responsibility. It is for each good and moral person to express indignation, to resist the tyrants and demagogues. Unless each person is ready to shake off moral indifference and fearfulness, the forces of evil will continue to prevail.

"And the Lord said unto Moses: Rise up early in the morning and stand [tall] before Pharaoh."

We are likewise commanded to stand tall before the Pharaohs of our times, to resist the agents of oppression, falsehood and injustice who undermine the fabric of our society and our world.

•••

2:13 – Go and see which is the right way to which one should cling:
R. Eliezer said: a good eye [generosity of spirit].
R. Yehoshua said: a good companion.
R. Yose said: a good neighbor.
R. Shimon said: one who considers the consequences.
R. Elazar said: a good heart.
Then he said to them: I prefer the answer of Elazar ben Arakh, for his view includes all of yours.

"A good heart..."

Our Mishnah makes the case that a good heart includes generosity of spirit, making good friends and neighbors, and considers future consequences. Scripture sets the tone for this thought. "More than all that you guard, guard your heart, for it is the source of life." [27] It makes perfect sense that the first paragraph of the Shema begins

---

26 *The Contract of Mutual Indifference*, Verso Books, New York and London, 1999, p. 120
27 Proverbs 4:23

this way "with all your heart." [28]

The Scriptural Book of Exodus refers to the heart as the seat of both the intellect and feelings, when it uses phrases such as "*hakham lev* – wise-hearted" and "*nediv lev* – a willing heart," when it speaks about the qualities of those who helped in the construction of the Tabernacle.

The Midrash agrees that the heart is the seat of understanding: "The heart sees, hears, speaks; the heart rejoices, weeps, breaks and rebels; the heart invents, suspects, desires, loves and hates; meditates, schemes and obeys." [29]

The importance of a good heart is crucial in so many different parts of Jewish tradition. In legislating regarding the offering of sacrificing offerings, the Mishnah teaches: "It is the same whether one offers much or little, so long as one directs one's heart to Heaven." [30]

In another passage the Talmud instructs: [31] that "the Blessed Holy One seeks the heart, and the barometer of greatness is devotion of the heart and not the amount of Torah that one studies, as it is written: 'But the Lord looks on the heart.'" [32]

Rabbi Samson Raphael Hirsch, in his commentary on this Mishnah, writes: "If...the 'heart' is 'good,' if the 'heart' is receptive only to the good and directed to the good alone, the *whole* man will be under the rule of the good; he will not be *capable* of desiring evil and will be ready for every good endeavor. Thus the characterization *lev tov* [a good heart] truly defines all the paths and devices that lead toward the good."

28 Deuteronomy 6:5
29 Midrash Ecclesiastes Rabbah 1:16
30 Tractate Menahot 13:11
31 Tractate Sanhedrin 106b
32 I Samuel 16:7

Work

1:10 – Love work.

This aphorism is one of many more scattered throughout rabbinic literature. The Sages deemed honest labor as honorable, moral and socially important. One who works for a living has personal dignity, and need not become dependent on charity. While the Sages considered work an important aspect of ordinary life, they deemed the Shabbat even higher, when no work was permitted. The Torah teaches in the Ten Commandments: "Six days shall you labor and do all your work, but the seventh day is a Sabbath unto the Lord your God; you shall not do any work." (1)

Rabbi Joseph Hertz comments on this Mishnah: "The slowness among Western nations to recognize the dignity of labor is no doubt due to the fact that, till quite recent times, classical literature monopolized the education of the governing classes among European peoples. As with the Greeks and Romans, idleness was for ages the mark of nobility." To the rabbis, "idleness leads to mental deterioration." (2)

The ancient rabbis considered their work in teaching as not appropriate to receive payment. They engaged in physical labor to support themselves. Hillel was a wood-cutter, Eliezer a farmer, Yehoshua ben Hananiah was a needle maker, Akiva was a shepherd, and Yohanan a cobbler

The Sages considered it vital for a father to teach his son a craft, a skilled profession, or otherwise he teaches him to steal. (3)

Following is a sample of the high regard in which the Sages deemed honest labor:

"Work brings honor to its master." (4)

"The merit of honest work surpasses even that of ancestral good deeds." (5)

"One who lives by his labors is superior to a God-fearing

1 Exodus 20:9-10
2 Tractate Ketubot 59b
3 Tractate Kiddushin 29a
4 Tractate Nedarim 49b
5 Midrash Tanhuma, Vayetze

person." [6]

"A person without a trade is compared to a vineyard without a fence or a pit without a guard rail." [7]

"It is better for a person to skin hides in the marketplace than to say, 'Such things are unbecoming for me.'" [8]

"Even Adam did not taste food until he had worked, as it is written, [9] 'The Lord God took the man and put him into the Garden of Eden to till it and keep it,' after which He said, 'Of every tree of the garden you may eat.' Even God did not cause His *Shekhinah* (Divine presence) to alight upon Israel until they had done work, as it is written, 'Let them make for Me a Sanctuary that I may dwell among them.'" [10]

"A person should not say, 'I stem from prestigious lineage – it is beneath me to do work.' Say to him: 'Fool! Your Creator has preceded you,' as in the verse: And God finished the **work** that He had done." [11]

In the *Birkat HaMazon* (Grace after Meals) we recite this sentence: "We pray to God to permit us never to need the gifts of humans, nor even to borrow from other Jews." It is important for our self-esteem and personal dignity to be able to support ourselves.

In modern times, with the development of Zionism and the birth of Israel, the return to working the soil, the establishment of farm colonies such as kibbutzim and moshavim, has spawned a resurrection of Jewish farmers. One of the leaders in this area was A. D. Gordon, [12] a Zionist ideologue and the spiritual force behind Labor Zionism. A philosopher who had never before engaged in hard physical work, came to Palestine at age forty-eight, became a day laborer and inspired the movement often called "*Dat HaAvodah*," the religion of labor. He strongly believed that the renewal of Jewish life in a renewed national movement and in a new country, must begin with hard work.

---

6 Tractate Berakhot 8a
7 Tosefta Kiddushin 1
8 Tractate Pesahim 113a
9 Genesis 2:15
10 Exodus 25:8; *Avot d'Rabbi Natan* 11
11 Zohar Hadash
12 1856-1922

The Workingman[13]

God bless the brawny arms of toil,
The noble hearts and royal hands,
That plow the plain and seed the soil,
And grow the grains of laughing lands!

King in the blessed vales of life
Where perfect pleasures first began,
May blessings come with raptures rife
To crown the humble workingman!

His kingdoms wave with bannered corn
And meadows bright with fairy bloom,
While duties of his heart are born
Where sylvan shadows hide the gloom.

Sweet Nature fills his heart with health,
While rustic warbles lead his soul
Where rill and fountain sing by stealth
And breezes soft with music roll.

He lives where simple wishes throng,
And give contentment to his breast,
While tender lullabies of song
Bring angel gladness to his rest.

No praises linger o'er his name
Where he in silence works apart,
And honor never links with fame
The modest glories of his heart.

He needs no kiss of royal crown
To wield the axe or guide the plow,
Or woo the smiles of heaven down
To cling in clusters on his brow.

13 Freeman Edwin Miller (1864-1951)

But in the sacred shine of love,
With humble deeds he lives his days,
And, drinking from the founts above,
He scatters gladness o'er his ways.

Proud monarch of the tattered vest,
Thy toil is fraught with greater gains
Than his that bleeds where warrior crest
Slays thousands on the battled plains!

Thy duty prompts to build, to grow,
The forest fell, the city plan
And scatter seeds of love below,
Where'er thou art, O, workingman!

•••

Work

by Steve Goodier
www.lifesupportsystem.com

Work sometimes has a bad reputation in our world. But there is something worse than work, and that is having no work to do. Even if we don't need the money, we still need to be productive. At least that is what Drs. Kathryn Rost and G. Richard Smith of the University of Arkansas say. After analyzing the mental health of heart attack survivors, they concluded that one factor which greatly reduced the chances of depression was going back to work.

And why not? For one thing, at work we are often around friends, and people with strong relationships will almost always fare better mentally. For another, we humans need to feel useful, and we are often most productive when we work.

The scholar Arthur Kroeger wrote in Quote magazine (August 1994) that his brother sometimes visited an Anabaptist colony in southern Alberta, Canada. During one visit he asked leaders how they dealt with the problem of misbehavior – when people rebelled against the colony's strict rules. He was told that these people were first asked to correct their behavior. If they did not respond, they would be given a stern "talking to."

"But what do you do when all else fails, when somebody stubbornly refuses to behave?" he pressed.

"Ah," came the reply, "if it comes to that, then we don't give him anything to do."

They are given no way to meaningfully contribute to their tight-knit community, nothing productive to do. For this colony, it is an effective behavior modification strategy.

Not having anything to do may work well when we enjoy some time away, but it makes for a poor lifestyle. Industrialist Henry Ford stated, "Work is our sanity, our self-respect, our salvation. So far from being a curse, work is the greatest blessing."

When I am unable to participate in some activity during working hours, I often turn it down by saying, "I have to work today." But that makes working sound like an unwelcome obligation. The truth is, I am grateful I have honest work to do and that I am able to do it. Even a feeling of exhaustion at the end of a busy day can't mask my satisfaction of having accomplished something useful. My work is an unexpected gift, and in that I am blessed.

Dale Carnegie gives this advice: "Are you bored with life? Then throw yourself into some work you believe in with all your heart, live for it, die for it, and you will find happiness that you had thought could never be yours." Even if that work is volunteer service, if you believe in what you're doing, your paycheck will be measured in satisfaction rather than money. And satisfaction is something money just can't buy.

The World-to-Come

2:21 The reward of the righteous is granted in the time to come.

4:21 – This world is like a lobby before the World-to-Come. Prepare yourself in the lobby so that you may enter the banquet hall.

Rashi's comment sums up very well the essence of this Mishnah. When a visitor to a king prepares himself for the visit, he arranges his hair and his clothing. In the same way we prepare ourselves for the World-to-Come through *Teshuvah* and good deeds. [1]

An important teaching from Tractate Mishnah Sanhedrin 10:1, a most appropriate introduction, recited ritually, prior to each chapter of Avot, is: "All Israel (every Jewish person) has a portion in the world-to-come." Rabbi Martin S. Cohen writes of this Mishnah: "To say that all Israel has a portion in the world-to-come is to say that Jewishness itself is a kind of transcendent quality that grants mission, depth, purpose, and dignity to life; that membership in the House of Israel is itself the key to overcoming the fear of death; and that purposefulness, tenacity, and determined perseverance in the service of God are the bedrock principles upon which Jewish existence has always rested and will always rest." [2]

An interesting comment on this Mishnah in Tractate Sanhedrin comes from the Hafetz Hayyim. [3] He interprets the phrase "has a portion" (Hebrew "*yesh lo helek*" to mean that we all have a portion, a part, a responsibility, in bringing the world-to-come, through our good deeds and righteous behavior (told to me by Rabbi Aaron Landes z"l, who heard it from his father, a rabbi who was ordained by the Hafetz Hayyim).

A comment similar to this Mishnah is found in Tractate Avodah Zarah 3a: "This world is similar to the eve of Shabbat, and the World-to-Come is like Shabbat. Prepare yourself on the eve of Shabbat and you will have food for Shabbat.

1 See on 4:13, comment c
2 *Pirkei Avot Lev Shalem*, p. xxxviii
3 Rabbi Yisrael Meir Kagan, d. 1933, Radin, Poland

This Mishnah enunciates a very important theological doctrine in Jewish tradition, that our days in this world are limited, [4] but the soul is eternal, and so our life in the World-to-Come is infinite.

The Talmud portrays a sublime existence in the next world: "The World-to-Come is not like this world. In the World-to-Come there is no eating, no drinking, no procreation, no business negotiations, no jealousy, no hatred, and no competition. Rather, the righteous sit with their crowns upon their heads, enjoying the splendor of the Divine Presence."

The author of this Mishnah formulated the important rabbinic doctrine that there is no physical reward for the fulfillment of the Divine mitzvot in this world.

Rabbi Abraham J. Twerski summarizes our Mishnah in these words: "We accept the reality that a person may have to put in a hard day's work, and except for brief interludes during the workday, he cannot relax until he comes home in the evening. Our earthly existence is out 'workday,' and except for brief periods of rest and tranquility, we are to engage in our work until we return to our true home in the Eternal World." [5]

Another interpretation of this Mishnah considers "the World-to-Come" some future time in today's world. If we prepared properly, and performed Teshuvah and good deeds, we would be able to live in a world without hatred, misogyny, xenophobia and war. The "World-to-Come" would be one in which "nation will not lift up sword against nation," [6] and "the lion will lie down with the lamb." [7]

There is an oft-quoted story of the Hafetz Hayyim that delivers an important message about the life of humans on earth.

> A wealthy businessman was passing through the Polish town of Radin. Not wanting to pass up the opportunity of seeing the leader of the generation, he went to visit the Hafetz Hayyim. Upon entering, he was struck by his sparsely furnished home. Unable to control himself, he blurted out, "Where is your furniture!?". The Hafetz Hayyim responded by asking where

4 See Psalm 90

5 *Visions of the Fathers*, p. 250

6 Isaiah 2:4

7 Isaiah 11:6

> was his furniture? The businessman, somewhat surprised, explained that he was only passing through. The Hafetz Hayyim explained that he too, is only passing through....

We mortals would have an entirely different attitude toward life if we agreed with the Hafetz Hayyim!

4:22 – Better one hour of repentance and good deeds in this world than all the life in the World-to-Come. Better one hour of bliss in the World-to-Come than the whole life of this world.

This Mishnah offers an unusual paradox. Rabbi Irving (Yitz) Greenberg explains it very well. "In this world you are a complete human being, a body and a soul. When you do good or repent from evil in this world there is a deeper, more totally human pleasure in these worldly activities. In this moment, when you are acting at the highest level, you receive a deeper fulfillment than you will in all of eternity – because there, only the soul dimension exists. On the other hand, the spiritual bliss is so sweet in the World-to-Come that one hour gives more satisfaction than all the physical pleasures of the entire mortal life."

Rabbi Joseph B. Soloveitchik cites this Mishna as capturing a profound, paradoxical truth of the Torah. [(8)] The religious person should focus totally on living this worldly life properly and fully. The Torah is all about living one's mortal flesh-and-blood life to the fullest. This is the true existence with God. On the other hand, we should be aware of and gladdened by the expectation of eternal joy in a future spiritual existence with God. (But this is like a bonus; it should not be the driving force of the religious life.) [(9)]

Another profound understanding of this paradoxical Mishnah is offered by Rabbi Shlomo P. Toperoff: [(10)] "Judaism, unlike Christianity, is not an other-worldly religion. We are not to become engrossed in the workings of the future life. 'The heavens belong to God, but the earth belongs to the sons of man.' [(11)] We are cautioned not to dabble in necromancy or spiritualism. The Torah forbids all

8 *Halakhic Man*, 30, 33ff., 41ff

9 *Sage Advice*, pages 217-218

10 Avot, p. 253

11 Psalm 19

speculations into the future but stresses this life, repentance and good deeds. There is much constructive work to be done on this earth. Thus the Law-giver clearly states, 'Keep My statutes and ordinances which, if a man does, he shall live by them.' [12] These words obviously refer to this world as the Rabbis underline by commenting, 'He shall not die by them'. This is what the Mishnah wishes to convey – one hour of repentance and good deeds on earth is richer than all the life in the World-to-Come, for the simple reason that one is unable to repent or to perform good deeds in the World-to-Come; this is reserved only for this world. However, one hour of serenity in the World-to-Come is better (more beautiful) than all the life in this world, which is referred to as *olam d'shikra*, a world of lies, envy, suspicion, jealousy, strife and war. The Hereafter is known as *olam haemet*, the world of truth, which is the seal of God Almighty. There, celestial bliss and perfect peace hold sway...."

12 Leviticus 18:5

Youth and Old Age

4:25 – When you learn as a child, what is it like? Like ink written on fresh paper. When you learn in old age, what is it like? Like ink written on erased paper.

4:26 – When you learn from the young, what is it like? Like eating unripe grapes or drinking unfermented wine straight from the vat. When you learn from the old, what is it like? Like eating ripe grapes and drinking old wine.

The first time I rode the Haifa Carmelit, (the subway on Mt. Carmel), during my year at Hebrew University (1962-3) and saw on the wall the quotation from Leviticus 19:32, "You shall rise before the aged," I knew that Israel was a different kind of country. And that Jewish tradition regarding honoring the elderly was not just a sentence from the Bible. Rashi's commentary, based on Tractate Kiddushin 32b on this verse, teaches that this mitzvah pertains not only to elders who are learned and wise, but as well to elderly people whose learning is minimal.

The Talmud in Tractate Berakhot 8b teaches: "Be mindful of the elderly who have forgotten their learning, not through their own fault, as it is written that the tablets and the broken tablets were placed in the ark together." (1)

The biblical book of Job testifies to the same idea: (2) "Is not wisdom found among the aged? Does not long life bring understanding?"

"Like eating unripe grapes...."

Rabbi Shmuly Yanklowitz comments: "The processes that transforms the humble grape into holy wine are similar to those that transform the unlearned student into the noble master." (3)

In addition to learning from wise elders, we also have an obligation to assist the elderly in every possible way. "We learn that

1 cf. Deuteronomy 10:1-2

2 Job 12:12

3 Pirkei Avot, page 267

everyone who is hospitable to an elderly person can be compared to welcoming the Divine Presence."[4]

I have been a member of AARP (American Association of Retired Persons) for several years. Their mission is "to empower people to choose how they live as they age." I receive frequent email appeals from AARP describing the sad state of millions of aging people. So many suffer from diseases such as Alzheimer's, dementia, Parkinson's, and more. We are told that by the year 2033 there will be over 77 million elderly in America. We need to do as much as we can to follow Jewish tradition's mandate "to rise before the aged," i.e., to rise to the challenge of financial and other means of support.

The biblical book Ecclesiastes tells us: "Appreciate your vigor in the days of your youth, before those days of sorrow come and those years arrive of which you will say, 'I have no pleasure in them.'"[5]

The Talmud laments the physical problems that arise from old age. Rabbi Yosei bar Kisma says: The two feet of one's youth are better than the three of old age, [when one walks with a cane]. Woe to the one who goes and does not come back. What is this referring to? Rav Ḥisda said: Youth. Rav Dimi said: Youth is a crown of roses; old age is a crown of thorns."[6]

Rabbi Nahman of Breslov taught that one can judge a country's prosperity by examining its treatment of the elderly. The High Holiday liturgy (the *Sh'ma Kolenu* prayer) enjoins us, "Cast me not out in old age, when my strength fails, do not forsake me."[7]

Rabbi Abraham Joshua Heschel warned that often the elderly see themselves as people who have "outlived [their] usefulness,... [and] feel as if [they have] to apologize for being alive. May I suggest that man's potential for change and growth is much greater than we are willing to admit, and that old age be regarded not as the age of stagnation but *as the age of opportunities for inner growth...* to deepen understanding and compassion...."[8]

Rabbi Marc D. Angel wrote this on youth and aging:

4 Genesis Rabbah 63:6

5 Ecclesiastes 12:1

6 Tractate Shabbat 152a

7 Psalm 71:9

8 "To Grow in Wisdom," *Judaism*, Spring 1977

Young and Old

When Moses demanded that Pharaoh release the Israelites so that they could go and worship God, he insisted: "We will go with our young and with our old, with our sons and with our daughters..." [9]

A Hasidic interpretation of Moses' words plays on the Hebrew: "*binareinu uvizkeineinu nelekh.*" Instead of translating "*binareinu*" as "with our young," it is translated as "with our youth." The meaning is: even as we advance in years, we carry our own youth within us i.e. we retain the enthusiasm and idealism of our younger days. We may appear to be old physically, but mentally and emotionally we are still energized by our own inner child.

In his book, *Late Bloomers*, Brendan Gill cites numerous examples of people who launched new and productive careers in their older years.

Oscar Hammerstein was 64 when he wrote the lyrics to The Sound of Music.

Michelangelo was 72 when he designed the dome of St. Peter's Basilica in Rome.

Frank Lloyd Wright was 91 when he completed work on the Guggenheim Museum.

A great many lesser known individuals have made remarkable achievements while elderly. What is their secret? They carry their youthfulness within! They are filled with wonder, with creativity; they want to keep learning and keep growing and keep testing their ideas.

Rabbi Dr. Abraham Twerski, in his book *Happiness and the Human Spirit*, advises readers: "The key is to think of self-fulfillment in terms of effort rather than outcome. All we can do is make the best effort possible." [10] It is all too easy to avoid undertaking new challenges due to fear of anticipated failure. People think: I'm too old, I will never finish this task, I don't have it within me to succeed any further. But this type of thinking is self-destructive. It saps life of meaning and happiness. Rather, one should rally the inner child to take a chance, to try to undertake something grand and challenging. Dr. Twerski wisely reminds us

9 Shemot 10:9

10 Twerski, *Happiness and the Human Spirit*, p. 91

that our responsibility is to exert our best effort and not to be overly daunted by the possible outcome.

The Hasidic interpretation focused on "*binareinu*;" but we should also pay attention to "*uvizkeineinu*." Although normally translated as "with our old," we might also understand this as a charge to each person, regardless of age, to imagine his/her older years yet to come. How would I deal with this problem if I were much older than I am now? What wisdom or experience could I bring to this new situation? If I were to look at my present life as though I were nearing life's end, how would I judge myself? What would I do differently?

It has often been said that no one, on his or her deathbed, looks back on life and says: I wish I had spent more time in my office! If we imagine ourselves to be looking back on our lives, we can often gain an important perspective on how to live our present lives more meaningfully.

When we seek freedom and the fulfillment of our spiritual nature, we need to draw on our inner youthfulness and on our anticipated elderly mature vision. Seeing our own lives through the prism of our past and our future helps us to live righteously and happily in our present.

"We will go with our young and with our old," said Moses to Pharaoh. Good advice, even today!

4:27 – Do not look at the vessel but at which it contains, for a new vessel may contain old wine, and an old vessel may not contain anything, even new wine.

The main thrust of this Mishnah seems to be contrary to the previous Mishnah, which claims that older teachers have more wisdom and experience than younger teachers. It is therefore a balance to that opinion. The point here is that while older teachers are more likely to have a better chance of having more wisdom and experience, it is not always so. There are young teachers who have mastered much wisdom and are thus excellent teachers. And there are older teachers whose knowledge is stale and perhaps out of date. In sum, do not let age be the only criterion for selecting a teacher.

A more general interpretation of this Mishnah is similar to the well-known adage, "Appearances are deceiving." Or, "Do not judge a book by its cover." The appearance of something does not always reveal its true contents.

In the Bible, God tells the prophet Samuel: [11] "For the Lord sees not as humans see: humans look on the outward appearance, but the Lord looks to the heart [the inside, the essence]."

The Sages warn that one must know both the appearance and the true essence of a scholar before passing judgment on one's authentic scholarly ability. "Any scholar whose inside is not like his outside [one who is insincere] is no scholar." [12]

The Hebrew expression for a sincere and genuine individual is poetic – "*tokho k'varo*". [13]

In Proverbs 31:30, we read of the importance of judging a person by their spiritual merit, rather than their appearance: "Charm is deceptive, and beauty is illusory, but a woman who fears the Lord is to be praised."

Rabbi Marc D. Angel makes a perceptive comment on this theme:

> In *Atlas Shrugged* by Ayn Rand, there is a passage about a boy who loved a great oak tree.
>
> "He felt safe in the oak tree's presence; it was a thing that nothing could change or threaten; it was his greatest symbol of strength."
>
> But one night, lightning struck the oak tree, splitting it in two. The next morning, the boy saw the fallen oak which had been rotten from within. In place of its core, it had hollowed out and had become frail.
>
> "The trunk was only an empty shell; its heart had rotted away long ago; there was nothing inside ... The living power had gone, and the shape it left had not been able to stand without it."
>
> Once the tree's core turned rotten, it was doomed to break when a storm would hit it.

11 I Samuel 16:7

12 Tractate Yoma 72b

13 Tractate Berakhot 28a

There are countries, communities, institutions – and people – who are like the oak tree in this story. They have the appearance of grandness and power; but they are rotting within. They gradually erode and become hollow. When they fall, people suddenly realize how badly they had been deceived by relying on quantity rather than quality.

In our world, it can be confusing to distinguish between a solid oak and an oak which is rotting at its core. Yet, if we cannot tell the difference, we are destined to great suffering and disillusionment.

The Torah reminds us not to judge success or strength by external numerical standards. The Israelites were not strong even though they multiplied in prodigious numbers. A hollow oak tree is not strong even if it is ancient and massive.

No nation, community, institution or individual can be deemed to be strong unless the inner life is healthy.

Glossary of Terms and Phrases

Amidah – Literally "standing," this term refers to the personal prayer at the center of every Jewish prayer service.

Am Ha-aretz – Literally "the people of the land, meaning "the peasantry, often used derisively to denote an ignoramus.

Avodah – "Work" or "service," often used to denote the Temple worship service.

Avot d'Rabbi Natan – A Jewish aggadic work probably compiled in the 8th and 9th century C.E., a homiletical exposition of Pirkei Avot.

Baal Shem Tov – Rabbi Israel ben Eliezer, known by the acronym, BESHT, a Jewish mystic and healer, regarded as the founder of Hasidic Judaism (Ukraine, 1700-1760).

Bartenura – Rabbi Ovadiah ben Abraham of Bartenura, (Italy, d. 1515), popular commentator on the Mishnah.

Bet Midrash – "House of study," a school or communal study hall.

Beit Mikdash – The Holy Temple in Jerusalem, destroyed by the Babylonians in 586 B.C..E., and afterwards rebuilt by King Herod, destroyed again by the Romans in 70 CE.

B'rakhah (plural b'rakhot) – blessing(s). Major statutory part of Jewish worship.

Derekh Eretz – Literally "the way of the land," often used as "good manners."

Eretz Yisrael – The Land of Israel

Gehinnom – A Hebrew term meaning "hell", often anglicized as "Gehenna."

Halakhah – Jewish law.

Hasidism – A religious movement that stressed religious piety, begun by Rabbi Israel Baal Shem Tov in the eighteenth century in Eastern Europe.

Kavanah – Literally "intention," the term is used to denote intentionality in the performance of religious rituals, especially prayer.

Keva – Literally "fixedness," the term is used to denote conformity to the fixed conventions of prayer.

Kohen Gadol – the High Priest.

Kitzur Shulhan Arukh – a summary of the Shulhan Arukh of Rabbi Joseph Karo, a work of Jewish law written by Rabbi Shlomo Ganzfried, in 1864.

Mahzor Vitry – A compendium of laws, prayers and liturgical poems, authored by Rabbi Simhah ben Shmuel of Vitry, France in the eleventh century.

Maharal – Hebrew acronym for "Moreinu HaRav Loew," Rabbi Judah Loew, an important Talmudic scholar and mystic (Prague, d. 1609).

Maimonides – Rabbi Moshe ben Maimon, commonly known by the acronym, Rambam (Rabbi Moshe ben Maimon), a Sephardic philosopher, one of the greatest scholars of the Middle Ages, commentator and philosopher, (b. Cordoba, Spain 1138, d. Fostat, Egypt, 1204).

Menorat HaMaor – Literally, "The Menorah of Light", title of an ethical work by Rabbi Isaac Aboab, end of fourteenth century, Spain.

Midah (plural Middot) – Positive character traits.

Midrash (plural Midashim) – Extensive interpretation of biblical texts; the term is usually applied to ancient rabbinic interpretation, especially from the third to ninth centuries in the Land of Israel and Babylonia.

Midrash Tanhuma – A collection of biblical legends, ascribed to Rabbi Tanhuma, eighth and ninth centuries.

Midrash Rabbah – Collection of Midrashim on the books of the Torah and the Five Megillot (Scrolls).

Rebbe – A Hasidic rabbi, or leader.

Rabbenu – Literally "my master," a rabbi or teacher.

Rashi – Acronym for "Rabbi Shlomo Yitzhaki," author of comprehensive commentaries on the Talmud and the Bible (Troyes, d. 1105).

Rav – Literally "master," a title for a rabbi or teacher of Torah.

Shekhinah –The rabbinic name for the feminine aspect of the Divine Presence.

Shtibl – Literally "little house," or "little room," usually a Hasidic synagogue, a center of prayer, study and social life.

Sadducees – A sect of Jews active in ancient Judea during the Second Temple period, from the second century BCE through the destruction of the Temple in 70 CE, representing an aristocratic, wealthy elite.

Tanna – A Rabbinic Sage whose views are recorded in the Mishnah, until 220 CE.

Tanya – An early work of Hasidic philosophy by Rabbi Shmeur Zalman of Liadi, the founder of Chabad Hasidism, first published in 1797.

Teshuvah – Literally "repentance," often meaning a return to traditional Judaism.

Tractate – One of the sixty-three volumes that comprise the Mishnah.

Tzaddik (plural Tzaddikim) – Literally, "a righteous person," a title given to people considered righteous.

Tzedakah – Literally "righteousness," usually referring to charity.

Tzibbur – Hebrew for community.

Yeshivah – Hebrew for academy, an educational institution that emphasizes traditional religious texts.

Yetzer HaTov – Hebrew for the good inclination. In rabbinic (Talmudic) doctrine, every human being has two inclinations, or instincts, one pulling toward goodness (*yetzer haTov*) and one (*yetzer haRa*) pulling toward evil.

Yetzer HaRa – Hebrew for the evil inclination.

Zohar – Literally Hebrew for "splendor" or "radiance," the foundational book of Jewish mystical thought known as Kabbalah; commentary on the mystical aspects of the Torah. It first appeared in Spain in the thirteenth century, ascribed to Rabbi Shimon bar Yohai, second century.

Bibliography

As A Tree By the Waters. Reuven P. Bulka. Feldheim. 1980.

Avot. Shlomo P. Toperoff. Jason Aronson. 1997.

Chapters of the Fathers. Samson Raphael Hirsch. Feldheim. 1972.

Hasidic Wisdom. ed. Simcha Raz, translated by Dov Peretz Elkins and Jonathan Elkins. Jason Aronson. 1997.

Pirkei Avot Lev Shalem. New York: The Rabbinical Assembly. 2019.

Pirke Avot. Joseph H. Hertz. Behrman House. 1945.

Pirke Avot. William Berkson. Jewish Publication Society. 2010.

Pirkei Avos Treasury. Mesorah Publications. 1995.

Pirkei Avos. Berel Wein. Shaar Press. 2003.

Pirkei Avot. Yosef Marcus. Kehot Publication Society. 2010.

Pirkei Avot: A Social Justice Commentary. Rabbi Shmuley Yankowitz. Central Conference of American Rabbis. 2018.

Sage Advice. Irving (Yitz) Greenberg. Maggid Publishers. 2016.

The Fathers According to Rabbi Nathan. Yale University Press. 1990.

The Koren Pirkei Avot. Jonathan Sacks and Marc D. Angel. Koren, 2015.

Visions of the Fathers. Abraham J. Tweski. Shaar Press. 1999.

Made in the USA
Monee, IL
04 December 2020

50855774R00090